*Citizeness Bonaparte*

*Lepagerie Bonaparte*

# CITIZENESS BONAPARTE

BY

IMBERT DE SAINT-AMAND

*TRANSLATED BY*

THOMAS SERGEANT PERRY

*WITH PORTRAIT*

**WILDSIDE PRESS**

MANHATTAN PRESS
474 W. BROADWAY
NEW YORK

# CONTENTS.

# CITIZENESS BONAPARTE.

## I.

### THE DAY AFTER THE WEDDING.

FOR two days the Viscountess of Beauharnais had borne the name of Citizeness Bonaparte. March 9, 1796 (19th Ventôse, year IV.), she had married the hero of the 13th Vendémiaire, the saviour of the Convention; and two regicides, Barras and Tallien, had been present as witnesses at the wedding. Her husband had spent only two days with her, and during these forty-eight hours he had been obliged more than once to lock himself up with his maps and to plead the urgency of an imperative task in excuse, shouting through the door that he should have to postpone love till after the victory. And yet, although younger than his wife, — she was nearly thirty-three, he only twenty-six, — Bonaparte was very much in love with her. She was graceful and attractive, although she had lost some of her freshness, and she had the art of pleasing her young husband; moreover, it is well known, as the Duke of Ragusa says in his Memoirs, "that in love it is idle to seek for reasons; one loves because one loves, and nothing is less capable of explanation and analysis than this feeling. . . . Bonaparte was in love in every meaning of the word. It was, apparently, for the first time; and he felt it with all the force of his character." But he had just been appointed commander-in-chief of the Army of Italy. He was obliged to turn his back on love, to fly to peril and glory. March 11, he wrote this letter to Letourneur, President of the Directory, to tell him of his marriage two days before: "I had commissioned Citizen Barras to inform the Executive Directory of my marriage with Citizeness Tascher Beauharnais. The confidence which the Directory has shown me in all circumstances makes it my duty to inform it of all my actions. This is a new tie of attachment to my country; it is an additional guarantee of my firm resolution to have no other interests than those of the Republic. My best wishes and respects."

The same day he left Paris, bidding farewell to his wife and to his little house in the rue Chantereine (later the rue de la Victoire), where his happiness had been so brief. Accompanied by his aide-de-camp, Junot, and his commissary-general, Chauvet, he carried with him forty-eight thousand francs in gold, and a hundred thousand francs in drafts, which were in part protested. It was with this modest purse that the commander of an army that had long been in want was to lead it to the fertile plains of Lombardy. He stopped at the house of Marmont's father, at Châtillon-sur-Seine, whence he sent Josephine a power of attorney to draw certain sums. March 14, at six in the evening, he stopped to change horses at Chanceaux, and from there he wrote a second letter, as follows: "I wrote to you from Châtillon, and I sent you a power of attorney to draw certain sums which are due me. Every moment takes me further from you, and every moment I feel less able to be away from you. You are ever in my thoughts; my fancy tires itself in trying to imagine what you are doing. If I picture you sad, my heart is wrung and my grief is increased. If you are happy and merry with your friends, I blame you for so soon forgetting the painful three days' separation; in that case you are frivolous and destitute of deep feeling. As you see, I am hard to please; but, my dear, it is very different when I fear your health is bad, or that you have any reasons for being sad; then I regret the speed with which I am separated from my love. I am sure that you have no longer any kind feeling towards me, and I can only be satisfied when I have heard that all goes well with you. When any one asks me if I have slept well, I feel that I can't answer until a messenger brings me word that you have rested well. The illnesses and anger of men affect me only so far as I think they may affect you. May my good genius, who has always protected me amid great perils, guard and protect you! I will gladly dispense with him. Ah! Don't be happy, but be a little melancholy, and above all, keep sorrow

from your mind and illness from your body: you
remember what Ossian says about that. Write to
me, my pet, and a good long letter, and accept a
thousand and one kisses from your best and most
loving friend."

At this time, Bonaparte was much more in love
with his wife than she was with him. He adored
her, while she was but moderately touched by the
fiery transports of a devoted husband who felt for
her a sort of frantic idolatry. She remained in
Paris, a little anxious, wondering whether the man
with whose fate she had bound herself was a madman
or a hero. At certain moments she felt perfect confidence in him; at others, she doubted. As a woman
of the old régime, she asked herself, " Was I wise
to marry a friend of young Robespierre, a Republican
general?" Bonaparte had fascinated Josephine; he
had not yet won her heart. His violent, strange
character inspired her, in fact, with more surprise
than sympathy. He bore no likeness to the former
courtiers of Versailles, the favorite types of nobility.
What in him was later to be called genius, was now
only eccentricity. Josephine was not very anxious
to go to join him in Italy. She loved the gutter of
the rue Chantereine as Madame de Staël loved that
of the rue du Bac. In Paris she was near her son
and daughter, her relatives and friends. She took
delight in the varied but brilliant society of the
Directory, which had acquired some of the old-time
elegance, and where her grace, distinction, and ami·

ability aroused general admiration. She saw with
pleasure the opening of a few drawing-rooms, which
seemed, as it were, to rise from the ashes; and she
was interested in the theatres and the social life in
which even the most indifferent woman finds some
charm.

Meanwhile, Bonaparte had reached Nice, and on
the 29th of March had taken command of the Army
of Italy. "There were to be seen," says the General
de Ségur, "fifty-two thousand Austrians and Sardinians and two hundred cannon, with abundant ammunition; and opposing them, thirty-two thousand
French, without pay, without provisions, without
shoes, who had sold half their belongings to buy
tobacco, or some wretched food. Most of them
lacked even bayonets. They had but sixty cannon,
and insufficient ammunition; the guns were drawn
by lame and mangy mules, the artillery-men went
on foot; and the cavalry was of no service, for the
men led rather than rode their horses." It was to
those men that the young general addressed this
famous proclamation: "Soldiers, you are poorly fed
and half-naked. The government owes you much,
but can do nothing for you. Your patience, your
courage, do you honor, but they bring you no advantage, no glory. I am about to lead you into the
most fertile plains in the world; there you will find
large cities and rich provinces; there you will find
honor, glory, and wealth. Soldiers of Italy, shall
you lack courage?"

At the moment of beginning this wonderful campaign, in which success seemed impossible, so great was the numerical superiority of the hostile armies, Bonaparte, though his ambition was so eager, did not forget his love. Before the first battle he wrote this letter, dated Porto Maurizio, the 14th Germinal (April 3, 1796): "I have received all your letters, but none has made such an impression on me as the last. How can you think, my dear love, of writing to me in such a way? Don't you believe that my position is already cruel enough, without adding to my regrets, and tormenting my soul? What a style! What feelings are those you describe! It's like fire; it burns my poor heart. My only Josephine, away from you, there is no happiness; away from you, the world is a desert in which I stand alone, with no chance of tasting the delicious joy of pouring out my heart. You have robbed me of more than my soul; you are the sole thought of my life. If I am worn out by all the torment of events, and fear the issue, if men disgust me, if I am ready to curse life, I place my hand on my heart; your image is beating there. I look at it, and love is for me perfect happiness; and everything is smiling, except the time that I see myself absent from my love."

Bonaparte, who was soon to be the prey of suspicion and jealousy, was now all confidence and rapture. A few affectionate lines from the hand he loved were enough to plunge him into a sort of ecstasy. "By what art," he goes on, "have you

learned how to captivate all my faculties? to con-
centrate in yourself my whole being? To live for
Josephine! That's the story of my life. I do everything to get to you; I am dying to join you. Fool!
I don't see that I am only going further away. How
many lands and countries separate us! How long
before you read these words, which but feebly express the emotions of the heart over which you
reign!" Alas! the sun of love is seldom for long
unclouded, and these rapturous whispers are soon followed by lamentations. That day he doubted neither
of his wife's fidelity, nor of her love, and yet he felt
the melancholy which is inseparable from grand
passions. "Oh! my adorable wife!" he wrote, "I
do not know what fate awaits me; but if it keeps
me longer from you, I shall not be able to endure it;
my courage will not hold out to that point. There
was a time when I was proud of my courage ; and
when I thought of the harm that men might do me,
of the lot that my destiny might reserve for me, I
looked at the most terrible misfortunes without a
quiver, with no surprise. But now, the thought
that my Josephine may be in trouble, that she may
be ill, and, above all, the cruel, fatal thought that
she may love me less, inflicts tortures on my soul,
stops the beating of my heart, makes me sad and
dejected, robs me of even the courage of fury and
despair. I often used to say, Man can do no harm
to one who is willing to die ; but now, to die without
being loved by you, to die without this certainty, is

the torture of hell; it is the vivid and crushing image of total annihilation. It seems to me as if I were choking. My only companion, you who have been chosen by fate to make with me the painful journey of life, the day when I shall no longer possess your heart will be that when for me the world shall have lost all warmth and all its vegetation. . . . I will stop, my sweet pet; my soul is sad, I am very tired, my mind is worn out, I am sick of men. I have good reason for hating them; they separate me from my love."

A man of Bonaparte's character never suffers long from melancholy. All at once the warrior reappears. He is suddenly aroused from his dream by the call of a trumpet, and he closes his letter thus: "I am at Porto Maurizio, near Oneglia; to-morrow I am at Albenga. The two armies are in motion, each trying to outwit the other. The most skilful will succeed. I am much pleased with Beaulieu; he manœuvres very well, and is superior to his predecessor. I shall beat him, I hope, out of his boots. Don't be anxious; love me like your eyes, but that's not enough, like yourself; more than yourself, than your thoughts, your mind, your life, your all. But forgive me, I'm raving; nature is weak, when one feels keenly, in him who loves you. To Barras, Sucy, Madame Tallien, my sincere regards; to Madame Château-Renard, the proper messages; to Eugene, to Hortense, my real love."

April 3, Bonaparte had perfect confidence in his

wife; the 7th, he suspects her: the 3d, he blames
her for writing too affectionately; the 7th, he blames
her for writing too coldly. He wrote to her from
Albenga, the 18th Germinal (April 7, 1796): "I
have received a letter which you interrupt to go,
you say, into the country; and afterwards you pre-
tend to be jealous of me, who am so worn out by
work and fatigue. Oh, my dear! . . . Of course, I
am in the wrong. In the early spring the country is
beautiful; and then, the nineteen-year-old lover was
there, without a doubt. The idea of wasting another
moment in writing to the man, three hundred leagues
away, who lives, moves, exists, only in memory of
you; who reads your letters as one devours one's
favorite dishes after hunting for six hours. I am
not pleased. Your last letter is as cold as friendship.
I find in it none of the fire which shines in your
glance, which I have sometimes fancied that I saw
there. But how absurd I am! I found your previous letters moved me too much; the emotions they
produced broke my rest and mastered my senses. I
wanted colder letters, but these give me the chill of
death. The fear of not being loved by Josephine,
the thought of her proving inconstant, of — But I
am inventing trouble for myself. When there is so
much that is real in the world, is it necessary to
devise more? You cannot have inspired me with
boundless love without sharing it, with your soul,
your thought, your reason; and no one can, in
return for such affection, such devotion, inflict a

deadly blow. . . . A memento of my only wife, and a victory, — those are my wishes; a single, complete memento, worthy of him who thinks of you at every moment."

The victories were about to follow, swift and amazing. April 12, it was Montenotte; the 14th, Millesimo. On the heights of Monte Zemolo, the army saw suddenly at its feet the promised land, the rich and fertile plains of Italy, with their splendid cities, their broad rivers, their magnificent cultivation. The rays of the dawn lit up this unrivalled view; on the horizon were to be seen the eternal snows of the Alps. A cry of joy broke from the ranks. The young general, pointing to the scene of his future conquests, exclaimed, "Hannibal crossed the Alps, and we have turned them!" April 22, the victory of Mondovi; on the 28th, the armistice of Cherasco with Piedmont. Bonaparte addressed this proclamation to his troops: "Soldiers, in fifteen days you have won six victories; captured twenty-one flags, fifty cannon, many fortified places; conquered the richest part of Piedmont; you have captured fifteen thousand prisoners, and killed and wounded ten thousand men. You lacked everything, you have supplied yourself with everything; you have gained battles without cannon; crossed rivers without bridges; made forced marches without shoes; often bivouacked without bread; the Republican phalanxes were alone capable of such extraordinary deeds. Soldiers, receive your due of thanks!"

Bonaparte sent his brother Joseph and his aide-de-camp Junot to Paris. The 5th Floréal (April 24, 1796), he wrote to his wife: "My brother will hand you this letter. I have a very warm friendship for him. He will, I hope, win yours; he deserves it. He is naturally of a very gentle character, and unfailingly kind; he is full of good qualities. I wrote to Barras asking that he be appointed consul in some Italian port. He wants to live in quiet with his little wife, out of the great whirl of important events. I recommend him to you. I have received your letters of the 16th and the 21st. You were a good many days without writing to me. What were you doing? Yes, my dear, I am, not jealous, but sometimes uneasy. Come quickly; I warn you that if you delay, you will find me ill. These fatigues and your absence are too much for me." Henceforth Bonaparte's keenest desire was to see his wife come to Italy. He begs and entreats her not to lose a moment. "Your letters," he goes on, "are the delight of my days, and my happy days are not very many. Junot is carrying twenty-two flags to Paris. You must come back with him; do you understand? It would be hopeless misery, an inconsolable grief, continual agony, if I should have the misfortune of seeing him come back alone, my adorable one. He will see you, he will breathe the air of your shrine, perhaps even you will grant him the singular and unappreciable favor of kissing your cheek, while I am alone, and very, very far away. But you will come,

won't you? You will be here, by my side, on my
heart, in my arms! Take wings, come, come! But
travel slowly; the way is long, bad, and tiresome. If
you were to upset or be hurt; if the fatigue — Come,
eagerly, my adorable one, but slowly."

King Joseph, in his Memoirs, thus speaks of his
and Junot's departure for Paris: "It was at Cherasco,
the 5th of Floréal, that my brother commissioned me
to set before the Directory his reasons for the speediest
possible peace with the King of Sardinia, in order to
isolate the Austrians in Italy. To his aide-de-camp
Junot he assigned the duty of presenting the battle-
flags. We left in the same postchaise and reached
Paris one hundred and twenty hours after our departure from Nice. It would be hard to form a notion of
the popular enthusiasm. The members of the Directory hastened to testify their content with the army
and its leader. Director Carnot, at the end of a
dinner at his house at which I was present, indignant
with the unfavorable opinion which Bonaparte's enemies expressed, declared before twenty guests that
they did him injustice, and opening his waistcoat, he
showed the portrait of the general, which he wore on
his heart, and exclaimed, 'Tell your brother that he
is there, because I foresee that he will be the saviour
of France, and that he must well know that in the
Directory he has only admirers and friends.'" Murat,
who had been sent from Cherasco, through Piedmont,
to carry the draft of the armistice to Paris, arrived
there before Joseph and Junot. Josephine asked of

them all the most minute details concerning her husband's success. In a few days he had stepped from obscurity to glory. Citizeness Bonaparte did not regret her confidence in the star of the man of Vendémiaire, and already in the Republic she held the position of a princess.

## II.

BONAPARTE'S glory had been, one might say, the work of an instant. The feeling in Paris was one of profound surprise. Even Josephine had been amazed at such swift and unexpected successes. Every one was asking for details about this young man who was known only from the part he played in the day of Vendémiaire, and whose origin was shrouded in mystery; but none knew anything more than how his name was pronounced and spelled. Of his family, his beginnings, his fortune, his character, the public knew absolutely nothing. But no one ever equalled Napoleon in the art of getting himself talked about. In his first proclamations to the army, in his first despatches to the Directory, we see this knowledge of effect which made the hero an artist. The Directory went to work to build him a pedestal with their own hands.

At first the *Moniteur* mentioned the success of the Army of Italy without especial emotion. It was on the last page of the number of May 10, 1796, that was printed the account of the reception of the flags

14

— a ceremony at which Josephine was present. The *Moniteur* spoke thus: "The Directory received to-day, in public session, twenty-one flags captured by the French Republicans from the Austrians and the Sardinians, at Millesimo, Dego, and Mondovi. The Minister of War, in presenting the officer who brought these trophies, made a speech in which he paid homage to the valor of this Army of Italy which, to the glory of finishing the campaign by its victories, adds that of opening it again by its triumphs, the precursors of a peace worthy of the French Republic. The officer then spoke with the virile accent and modest air which characterize the heroes of liberty. In the name of his fellow-soldiers he swore that they would shed the last drop of their blood in defence of the Republic, in behalf of the enforcement of the laws, and of the support of the Constitution of 1795. The President of the Directory replied with an emotion which rendered the dignity of his words more touching. He offered the brave officer a sword and gave him a fraternal kiss. This session, which lasted but half an hour, presented a spectacle as imposing as it was moving. The sounds of military music added to the general enthusiasm, which frequently manifested itself by cries of 'Long live the Republic!'"

In her interesting Memoirs, the Duchess of Abrantès speaks of the effect produced on that day by Madame Bonaparte and Madame Tallien, who were two of the principal ornaments of this patriotic festival. " Madame Bonaparte," she says, "was still charming. . . . As for Madame Tallien, she was then in the flower of her wonderful beauty. Both were dressed after the fashion of antiquity, which was at that time regarded as the height of elegance, and as sumptuously as was possible for the middle of the day. Junot must surely have been very proud to give his arm to two such charming women, when they left the Directory after the reception. Junot was then twenty-five years old: he was a handsome young man, and had a most striking martial air; on that day he wore a magnificent uniform of a colonel of hussars (the uniform of Berchini), and all that the richness of such a dress could add to his fine appearance had been employed to make the young and brave messenger, who was still pale from the wounds which had stained those flags, worthy of the army he represented. On leaving, he offered his arm to Madame Bonaparte, who had precedence as the wife of his general, especially on this formal occasion; the other he gave to Madame Tallien, and thus he descended the staircase of the Luxembourg." Would not Junot, as colonel of hussars, with Josephine on one arm and Madame Tallien on the other, on the staircase of the palace of Maria de' Medici, make a charming subject of a *genre* picture? The Duchess of Abrantès describes the excitement of the crowd, who were anxious to see the young hero and the two fashionable beauties. " The throng," she says, " was numberless. They surged and pressed for a better

view. 'See; there's his wife! that's his aide-de-
camp! How young he is! And how pretty she is!
Long live General Bonaparte!' shouted the people.
'Long live Citizeness Bonaparte! She is kind to the
poor!' 'Yes, yes,' said a fat marketwoman; 'she is
certainly Our Lady of the Victories.'"

The poet Arnault, in his *Souvenirs of a Sexagenarian*, also describes the effect produced by Josephine's beauty on this occasion. Madame Bonaparte,
who was much admired, shared the sceptre of popularity with Madame Tallien and Madame Récamier.
"With these two women for her rivals," says
Arnault, "although she was less brilliant and fresh,
yet, thanks to the regularity of her features, the wonderful grace of her figure, and her agreeable expression, she too was beautiful. I still recall them all
there, dressed in such a way as to bring out their
various advantages most becomingly, wearing beautiful flowers on their heads, on a lovely May day, entering the room where the Directory was about to
receive the battle-flags: they looked like the three
spring months united to celebrate the victory." The
young poet, who more than once had the honor of
escorting Josephine, was very proud to accompany
her and Madame Tallien to the first performance of
Lesueur's *Télémaque* at the Théâtre Feydeau. "I
will confess," he says, "that it was not without some
pride that I found myself seated between the two
most remarkable women of the time, and it is not
without some pleasure that I recall the fact: those

feelings were natural for a young man enthusiastic for beauty and for glory. It was not Tallien whom I should have loved in his wife, but it was certainly Bonaparte whom I admired in his."

At that time Bonaparte passed for a perfect Republican. He had written to the Directory, May 6: "For a long time nothing has been able to add to the esteem and devotion which I shall display at every opportunity for the Constitution and the government. I have seen it established amid the most disgusting passions, all tending equally to the destruction of the Republic and of the French commonwealth; I was even able by my zeal and the force of circumstances, to be of some use at its beginning. My motto shall always be to die in its support."

The Directors thought that a general who expressed such an ardent devotion to Republican ideas ought to receive every encouragement and all praise. With no suspicions of the conqueror's future conduct, they were anxious to adorn themselves, as it were, with his victories, and to make them redound to the glory of their government. Hence the ceremony of May 10 seemed insufficient; they decided that the new festivals should be more brilliant and impressive. It was on the 10th of May, the day when the Directory formally received the flags captured in the first victories, that Bonaparte won the battle of Lodi, — a glorious day that made a deep impression on the imagination of the populace. None thought of anything except of the bridge over which, in spite of the

fire of the enemy converging on its long and narrow
path, the young hero had led his grenadiers at the
double quick.  They already had begun to call him
infallible and irresistible.  May 15, he made his triumphal entry into Milan.

The Directory was entranced.  Its Commissary
General of the Army of Italy, Salicetti, had written,
May 11: "Citizens Directors, immortal glory to the
brave Army of Italy!  Gratitude for the chief who
leads it with such wise audacity!  Yesterday will be
famous in the annals of history and of war. . . .  The
Republican column having formed, Bonaparte passed
through the ranks.  His presence filled the soldiers
with enthusiasm; he was greeted with incessant cries
of 'Long live the Republic!'  He had the charge
sounded, and the men rushed on the bridge with
the speed of lightning."

To celebrate these new triumphs, the Directory
prepared a festival, half patriotic, half mythological,
one more Pagan than Christian, in which reminis-
cences of Plutarch mingled with those of Jean
Jacques Rousseau; one in which, besides the heroic
feeling of the time, there found expression its fondness for declamation and its love of extravagant
language.  The "Festival of Gratitude and of the
Victories" (such was its official title) was celebrated
at the Champ de Mars, the 10th Prairial, Year IV.,
May 29, 1796.  In the middle of the Champ de Mars,
which was called also the Champ de la Réunion,
there had been raised a platform about twelve

feet high. There led to it four flights of steps, each about sixty feet broad. At the foot of the steps were lions, " the symbol of force, courage, and generosity," according to the *Moniteur.* The circle describing the limits of the space devoted to the ceremony was formed by cannon which served as barriers; between the cannon, flags were arranged which were connected by festoons of flowers. On a pedestal in the middle of the rising ground appeared the statue of Liberty seated amid various military trophies, with one hand resting on the Constitution, and in the other holding a wand, on the top of which was William Tell's cap. Perfumes were burning in antique tripods placed about the statue. On one side arose a high tree on which were hung, like trophies, the captured battle-flags. Near by, on pedestals, stood the Victories, like figures of Fame. Each one of them held in one hand a palm, and in the other a military trumpet raised to her lips. Finally, on an altar, were oak and laurel leaves which the Directors were to distribute in the name of the grateful country.

At ten in the morning, a salvo of artillery announced the beginning of the festival. The slopes of the Champ de Mars were covered with tents. The Parisian National Guard, with its arms and banners, marched forward in fourteen sections, representing the fourteen armies of the Republic. To each one of these fourteen sections was added a certain number of disabled veterans or wounded soldiers, and care had been taken to place them in the section representing the army in which they had received their wounds. Carnot spoke first, as President of the Directory. His speech was, so to speak, a military eclogue. The former member of the Committee of Public Safety celebrated military glory after the fashion of a pastoral. He blew in turn the trumpet and the shepherd's pipe. Sensibility mingled with warlike ardor. It was a sermon of a Tyrtæus. Few documents so well reflect the ideas and tastes of the society of that time as this speech, which is full of words of war, and, at the same time, of humanity. It begins thus: " At this moment, when nature seems to be born anew, when the earth, adorning itself with flowers and verdure, promises us rich harvests, when all creatures announce in their language the beneficent Intelligence which makes over the universe anew, the French people gather, in this solemn festival, to render fitting homage to the talents and the virtues loved by the country and by every human being. What day could more fitly unite all hearts? What citizen, what man, can be insensible to the feeling of gratitude? We exist only by means of a long series of benefits, and our life is but a continual interchange of services. Feeble, without support, our parents' love watches over our infancy. They guide our first steps; their patient solicitude aids the development of our members; from them we receive our first notions of what we are ourselves and of what is out-

side of us." After this exordium comes the usual
praise of sensibility, the fashionable term, which the
most ferocious of the Terrorists, Robespierre himself,
had employed with so much emphasis. "Sensibility,"
said Carnot, "does not confine itself to the narrow
sphere of the family circle; it goes forth to find the
needy in his hovel, and pours into his breast the balm
of aid and consolation, and though already rewarded
for its benevolence by the feeling of benevolence, it
receives a further recompense from gratitude. Humanity, how delicious is thy practice! how pitiable
the greedy soul who knows thee not!"

After this dithyramb in honor of nature, the family,
and sensibility, come martial descriptions; as after
the harp, the trumpet. "The new-born Republic
arms its children to defend its independence; nothing
can stem their impetuosity: they ford rivers, capture
retrenchments, scale cliffs. Then, after a host of
victories, they enlarge our boundaries to the barriers
which nature itself has set, and pursue over the ice
the fragments of three armies: there, they are about
to exterminate the hordes of traitors and of brigands
vomited forth by England, they punish the guilty
leaders and restore to the Republic their brothers, too
long lost; here, crossing the Pyrenees, they hurl
themselves from the mountain top, overwhelming
every obstacle, and are stopped only by an honorable
peace; then, scaling the Alps and the Apennines,
they dash across the Po and the Adda. The ardor of
the soldier is seconded by the genius and the audacity

of his leaders, who form their plans with wisdom and carry them out with energy, — now arranging their forces with calmness, now plunging into the midst of dangers at the head of their companions."

Carnot concluded his speech with an expression of gratitude to the soldiers of the Republic. "Accept," he exclaimed, "accept this solemn testimonial of national gratitude, O armies of the Republic! . . . Why is nothing left but your memory, ye heroes who died for liberty? You will at least live forever in our hearts; your children will be dear to us. The Republic will repay to them what it owes you; and we have come here to pay the first, in proclaiming your glory and its recognition. Republican armies! represented in this enclosure by some of your members, ye invincible phalanxes whose new successes I see in the future, advance and receive the triumphal crowns which the French people orders to be fastened to your banners." •

Later, there was dancing on the Champ de Mars until nightfall. In the evening there was a great Republican banquet at which was sung a hymn, half patriotic, half convivial, composed for the occasion by the poet Lebrun, — Pindar Lebrun, as he was then called. It ran as follows: —

"O day of undying memory,
Adorn thyself with our laurels!
Centuries, you will find it hard to believe
The prodigies of our warriors.
The enemy has disappeared in flight or has drunk the black wave.

" Under the laurels, what charms has Bacchus?
  Let us fill, my friends, the cup of glory
  With a nectar fresh and sparkling !
  Let us drink, let us drink to Victory,
  Faithful mistress of the French.

" Liberty, preside over our festivities ;
  Rejoice in our brilliant exploits !
  The Alps have bowed their heads,
  And have not been able to defend the kings.
The Eridanus recounts to the seas our swift conquests," etc., etc

We have seen what was going on in Paris.    What
had happened at Milan ?

## III.

THE young and valiant army which had just made its triumphant entrance into Milan was full of ardor, fire, and enthusiasm. All were young, — the commander, the officers, and the men, — as were their ideas, feelings, and hopes. These short men of the South, with their sunburned faces, their expression of wit and mischief, their eyes of fire, had a proud and free air. They had the merits of the French Revolution without its faults. They were brave and kind, terrible and generous, magnificent in the battle, and gay and amusing on the day after the victory. Full of imagination, rather inclined to talking and bragging, but yet so worthy of respect for their heroism, their self-denial, their unselfishness; they were not ambitious for themselves, but only for their country. They had no jealousy of one another, and did not care for rank or money. The military career was not their trade, but a vocation, a passion. They preferred their ragged uniforms to the luxury of a millionnaire. They despised everything which was not military. Not only had they no fear of danger,

25

they loved it, and lived in it as if it were their element. In the redoubt of Dego, Bonaparte exclaimed, " With twenty thousand such men, one could march through Europe." A Gascon grenadier answered aloud, " If the little corporal will always lead us in that way, I promise that he will never see us in retreat." Since Cæsar's legionaries there had been nothing seen that could be compared with Bonaparte's soldiers. They were very happy at Milan. They who had so long been without shoes, —

"Barefooted, without bread, deaf to cowardly alarms,
All marched to glory with the same step,"—

were now well nourished, well clad and shod. Good shoes are a great happiness to a poor soldier. They were in this city, which is a sort of earthly paradise, with its magnificent marble cathedral, its beautiful women, its enchanting views. The city is surrounded by a remarkably fertile country : meadows, woods, fields, gilded by the sun ; in the distance appears the huge chain of the Alps, the summits of which, from Monte Viso and Monte Rosa as far as the mountains of Bassano, are covered with snow all the year round. The air is so pure and limpid that the nearest points of the Alpine chain, though really a dozen or fifteen leagues away, seem scarcely more than three. The soldiers gazed with rapture at this glowing panorama, at the rich fields of Lombardy, this promised land ; at gigantic Monte Viso, which had so long risen over their heads, and now they were to see the sun set behind it.

Bonaparte entered Milan May 15, 1796. He found there a large force of the National Guard, wearing the Lombard colors, — green, white, and red. Under the command of a great nobleman of the city, the Duke of Serbelloni, it was drawn up in line along his path. Cheers filled the air. Pretty women were looking out from every window. When Bonaparte reached the Porta Romana, the National Guard presented arms before him. With a large detachment of infantry in advance, and surrounded by his guard of hussars, he went on as far as the Place in front of the Archducal Palace, where he was quartered, and there was served a dinner of two hundred plates. A liberty-tree was set out in the square, amid shouts of "Hurrah for Liberty! Long live the Republic!" The day closed with a very brilliant ball, at which appeared several ladies of the city, wearing the French national colors.

The same day, one of Bonaparte's aides-de-camp, Marmont, who was later Duke of Ragusa, wrote to his father: "Dear Father, we are to-day in Milan. Our triumphal entry recalled the entrance of the ancient Roman generals into Rome when they had deserved well of the country. Milan is a very fine city, large and populous. Its inhabitants are thoroughly devoted to the French, and it is impossible to express all the signs of affection they have given us. . . . It is easy to forget all the fatigues of a war as hot as this has been, when victory is our reward. Our successes are really incredible. They make

General Bonaparte's name forever famous, and it is perfectly clear that we owe them to him. Any one else in his place would have been beaten, and he has gone on simply from one triumph to another. . . . This campaign is the finest and most brilliant that has ever been known. It ought to be recorded and read. It is full of instruction, and those who can understand it will get great profit from it. Such, dear father, is a faithful picture of our situation."

That evening Bonaparte asked his aide-de-camp, " Well, Marmont, what do you suppose people are saying about us in Paris? Are they satisfied?" " They must be filled with admiration for you." " They haven't seen anything yet," replied Bonaparte; " there are still greater successes for us in the future. Fortune has not smiled on us to-day for me to despise her favors; she is a woman, and the more she does for me, the more I shall demand of her. . . . In our time, no one has devised anything great; I must set an example."

Bonaparte possessed to a wonderful degree the art of striking the imagination. One would have said that in him was revived one of the great men of Plutarch. His genius, fed on the history of the ancients, transported antiquity into modern times. All his words and actions, even when they appeared most simple, were arranged for effect. He thought continually of Paris, as Alexander used to think of Athens. The feeling which he was anxious to inspire was a mixture of admiration and surprise. With an unrivalled audacity, and the adventurous spirit of a gambler who stakes everything for everything, he united a knowledge of the human heart most astounding in a man of his age. Nothing is rarer than this combination of a boundless imagination with a positive and scheming mind. There were in Bonaparte two different and complementary persons,— the poet and the practical man. He dreamt and he acted; he adored at the same time Ossian and mathematics; he passed from the wildest visions to the most precise realities; from the sublimest generalities to the humblest and most trivial details. It is this harmony between generally incompatible qualities that makes him such an original figure.

The general's great merit lay in perceiving at once what he could do with such men as he had under his command. So humdrum a society as ours cannot easily understand heroic times when the richest banker is inferior to a simple sub-lieutenant, when the military spirit was every day calling forth fabulous exploits. Bonaparte's soldiers believed in him, and he believed in them. The strength of this unrivalled army lay in this, that they had confidence. The French are knights by birth. The Republic, far from changing their character, only made them more enthusiastic. As soon as they had received their baptisms of fire, the Jacobins became paladins, the Sans Culottes found themselves filled with the aspirations of the Crusaders. The companions of Charlemagne or of Godfrey of Bouillon were not

braver or more ardent. What an irresistible fire
there was in that revolutionary chivalry, the nobility
of a day, which already effaced the old coats of arms,
and when applauded by the aristocracy of Milan, it
could proudly say, like Bonaparte, " One grows old
quickly on the battle-field."

Stendhal knew how to describe most accurately
this glorious poverty of the heroes of the Army of
Italy, in the characteristic anecdote which he tells
of one of the handsomest of its officers, a M. Robert.
When he reached Milan, in the morning of May 15,
M. Robert was invited to dinner by a marchioness, to
whose house he had been billeted. He dressed himself with great care, but what he needed was a good
pair of shoes; of his own, only the uppers were left.
These he fastened very carefully with little, well-
blacked cords; but, I repeat, the shoes had no soles at
all. He was received most cordially by the marchioness, and he found her so charming, and was in such
uneasiness lest his poverty should have been detected
by the lackeys in magnificent livery who were waiting
on the table, that when he rose, he dropped a six
franc piece into their hands: it was every penny he
had in the world.

At that time, society was not thoroughly honey-
combed with corruption; there were great ladies who
loved for the sake of love, and money was not the
sole attraction. The desire of pleasure was most keen
in those days when one counted on a short life. The
deadlier the battles, the greater the eagerness for

amusement. The more they braved death, the more feverishly they pursued what makes life agreeable. What could be bought for money they did not care for; but what could not be bought, like love and glory, they sought with the utmost ardor.

Moreover, from the moment they entered Milan, the soldiers enjoyed a comfort to which they had long been strangers. They began to grow fat; they had good bread and meat to eat, and good wine to drink; they changed their rags for new uniforms supplied by the city. Monday, May 16, Bonaparte received the oath of allegiance from the city authorities: that evening there was a concert in the theatre of La Scala, which was brilliantly lit. The 18th, a new liberty-tree was planted, and a national feast was announced in the name of the Society of the People, in a decree dated Year I. of the Lombard Republic. The 19th, the city was illuminated, and everywhere was posted this proclamation, signed by Bonaparte and Salicetti: " The French Republic, which has sworn hatred to tyrants, has at the same time sworn fraternity with the people. . . . The despot who so long held Lombardy beneath his yoke did great harm to France; but the French know that the cause of kings is not that of their people. It is sure that the victorious army of an insolent monarch would spread terror throughout a defeated nation; but a republican army, compelled to make war to the death against the kings it combats, promises friendship to the people whom its victories deliver from tyranny."

Bonaparte seemed happy, yet even at the moment of his victory he was suffering. Stendhal has said: " Seeing this young general under the handsome triumphal arch of the Porta Romana, it would have been hard for even the most experienced philosopher to guess the two passions which tormented his heart." These were the hottest love excited by madness to jealousy, and anger due to the determination of the Directory. The very evening before his victorious entry into Milan, Bonaparte, unknown to any of those about him, had sent to Paris his resignation. He had just been informed by the Directory, that henceforth the Army of Italy was to be divided into two armies, one of which, that of the South, was to be confided to him, and was to set forth to conquer the southern part of the Peninsula; while the other, that of the North, was to be commanded by General Kellerman. Bonaparte perceived that this arrangement robbed him of his glory, and would destroy his power and fame. May 14, he wrote to the Directory a letter containing this passage: "I regard it as very impolitic to divide the Army of Italy; it is equally unfavorable to the interests of the Republic to set it under two different generals. I have conducted the campaign without consulting any one; I should have failed if I had been compelled to adapt myself to another's methods. I have gained some advantages over greatly superior forces, when I was in absolute need of everything, because, confiding in your trust in me, my march was as swift as my thought. . . . I feel that it takes much courage to write to you this letter; it exposes me to the charge of ambition and pride. But I owe to you this statement of my feelings." The same day he wrote privately to Carnot a letter which closed thus : " I am very anxious not to lose, in a week, two months of fatigue, toil, and danger, and also not to be fettered. I have begun with some glory, and I desire to continue to be worthy of you. Believe, moreover, that nothing will diminish the esteem which you inspire in all who know you."

Thus the successful general, at the very beginning of his career, was threatened with the loss of the command which had brought him so much renown. Possibly it was not this thought which most sorely wrung his passionate heart. He had besought his wife to join him, and yet she had not come. Days and weeks passed, but he received no news of her starting. Perhaps, — he thought in his heart, — perhaps she does not come because she is detained in Paris by love for some one else. This tormenting thought marred the joy of his triumph.

# IV.

MADAME DE RÉMUSAT says, in her curious Memoirs: "I ought to speak about Bonaparte's heart; but if it is possible to believe that a being like us in every other respect should yet be destitute of that part of our nature which inspires us with the need of loving and being loved, I should say that when he was created, his heart was probably forgotten; or else, perhaps, that he knew how to repress it completely. He was too anxious for his own fame to be hampered by an affectionate feeling of any sort. He scarcely recognized the ties of blood, the rights of nature." This opinion seems to us strangely exaggerated. Doubtless ambition and the lust of glory finally prevailed over every other feeling in this man's soul. Yet we are not justified in saying, with Lamartine: —

"No human feeling beat beneath thy thick armor.
　Without hate and without love, thou didst live to think.
　Like an eagle, reigning in a solitary heaven,
　Thou hadst but a glance wherewith to measure the earth,
　　　And talons to embrace it."

34

Whatever the poet may say, Napoleon knew both hate and love. Whatever power a man may obtain. he cannot rise outside of humanity. Heroes and rulers, unable to satisfy that void which is called the heart with the triumphs of glory and ambition, they feel the need of personal happiness, like humble citizens; and they are often more elate over a word, a glance, a smile, than over all the splendor of their greatness and all the intoxication of victory. To deny Bonaparte's passionate love for Josephine in 1796 would be to deny the evidence. All those who were in his company at the time agree in bearing witness to this feeling. His secretary, Bourrienne, and his aides-de-camp, Marmont and Lavalette, his friend, the poet Arnault, were all equally struck by it. Marmont has said, in the part of his Memoirs devoted to the first Italian campaign: "Bonaparte, however occupied he may have been with his greatness, the interest entrusted to him, and with his future, had nevertheless time to devote to feelings of another sort; he was continually thinking of his wife. He desired her, and awaited her with impatience. . . . He often spoke to me of her, and of his love, with all the frankness, fire, and illusion of a very young man. Her continual postponement of her departure tormented him most grievously; and he gave way to feelings of jealousy, and to a sort of superstition which was a marked trait of his character. During a trip we made together at this time, to inspect the places in Piedmont that had fallen into our hands, one morning, at Tortona, the glass in front of his wife's portrait, which he always carried with him, broke in his hands. He grew frightfully pale, and suffered the keenest alarm. 'Marmont,' he said to me, 'my wife is either ill or unfaithful.'"

The excitement of war, so far from distracting Bonaparte from his love, rendered him only more ardent, eager, and enthusiastic. His impetuous nature could easily be moved by two passions at once, — by his love for his wife and his love of glory. The perpetual restlessness in which he lived made him a ready victim of the tender passion. In his desires there was an impatient, imperious, despotic quality. He could no more understand a woman's resistance than the failure to win a victory. He summoned Josephine; consequently, Josephine must hasten to him. Rather a lover than a husband, he had passed but forty-eight hours with her since their marriage, and all his sentiment had been aroused, without being satiated. The careless creole, who was unaccustomed to such transports, was perhaps more surprised than delighted by them.

M. Lanfrey has, in our opinion, given a very exact account of the different feelings of Josephine and her husband at this time, when he says, speaking of Napoleon's love for his wife: "In this love, which has been said to be the only one that touched his heart, all the fire and flame of his masterful nature showed itself. As for Josephine, in his presence she felt more embarrassment and surprise than love. The very genius which she saw glowing in his piercing and commanding eye exercised over her amiable and indolent nature a sort of fascination which she could not feel without a secret terror, and before yielding to it she wondered more than once whether the extraordinary self-confidence manifested in the general's most insignificant words might not be merely the result of a young man's presumption which might easily be destined to bitter disappointment."

Without doubt she was much flattered by Bonaparte's early successes, but, as Marmont points out, "she preferred enjoying her husband's triumphs in Paris to joining him." To her it was a serious matter to leave her children, her relatives, and her life in Paris, so admirably suited to her kindly, amiable, affectionate but withal somewhat light and frivolous nature. She liked that amusing and brilliant city, which, though still shorn of its former animation, was yet busy and charming. The theatres, which at that time were crowded, the drawing-rooms, which were slowly reopening, the elegance and courtly manners of the old régime, which were appearing anew, the palace of the Directory, — all these things pleased Josephine. As the poet Arnault says in his *Souvenirs of a Sexagenarian:* "The Terror, which had so long made Paris its prey, was followed by a period of almost absolute indifference with regard to everything except pleasure. By enjoyment of the present, society anticipated the future and made up for the past. The Luxembourg, of which the five Directors had taken possession, had already become what will always be the place where authority rules, — a court; and since it was open to women, they had introduced softer manners. The Republicans began to abandon their brutal ways and to see that gallantry was not wholly incompatible with politics, and that indeed skill might be shown in employing it as a way of retaining power. The entertainments in which ladies resumed the empire from which they had been driven during the long reign of the Convention, showed clearly that those in power thought less of destroying the old customs than of imitating them.

Besides, all Madame Bonaparte's friends never tired of telling her that her place was not in Italy; that the war had only begun; that she should leave the victorious general entirely to his military affairs, his campaign plans, his strategy; and that a young wife was not intended to take part in all the tumult of a fight or the disorderliness of a camp. M. Aubenas, in his excellent *History of the Empress Josephine*, says: "Madame Bonaparte has been severely criticised for not hastening to Italy in the month of April, at her husband's first summons, before the victory of Lodi and the subjection of Lombardy; but frankly, it was only her husband, whose genius inspired him with confidence in his success, whose love scorned every obstacle, who could have imagined such excessive haste. Certainly, in the early wars of the Republic, it was not usual to see the general's wives following the armies. Prudence and regulations, for obvious reasons, forbade such a course. We have no intention of carving an image of Josephine as a Roman heroine. To start out thus at once to face all the fatigues and uncertainty of a great war, to bivouac in the Italian towns, in a word, to undertake the campaign, was an extreme demand to make of this creole nature in which indifference was a fault as well as a charm."

Bonaparte could not tolerate such hesitation. In order to persuade his wife to come to him, he wrote a mass of letters, each more urgent than its predecessor. The men of the old régime, who had paid attention to Josephine, would probably have smiled at the style and the manner. That a husband should love his wife in that way would probably have seemed to them a little vulgar. To be sure, they used to read the *Nouvelle Héloïse*, but nevertheless they had not formed the habit of writing to their legal wives tirades and hyperboles in imitation of Jean Jacques. Alexander de Beauharnais had not prepared his wife for love of this sort, which the fashionable society of Versailles might have regarded as proper for lovers, but absurd from a husband to his wife. Madame Bonaparte did not take seriously her husband's torrents of passion. As Arnault says: "Murat gave to Madame Bonaparte a letter in which the young hero urged her speedy departure; she showed me this letter, as well as all he had written since leaving her, and all expressed the most violent passion. Josephine found a good deal of amusement in this feeling, which was not devoid of jealousy. I seem to hear her once more reading one passage in which her husband, in the effort to allay the suspicions which evidently tortured him, said, 'But suppose it true! Fear Othello's dagger!' I hear her say with her creole accent, while she smiles, 'How funny Bonaparte is!'"

Madame de Rémusat, unfavorable as she is to Napoleon, and with every disposition to deny him any trace of tenderness, is nevertheless compelled to make this acknowledgment in her Memoirs: "For Josephine he felt some affection, and if he was at times moved, it was only for her and by her. Even a Bonaparte cannot escape every feeling." Yes; Bonaparte knew the force of love. I ask no other proof than the letter full of real eloquence and ardent passion which he wrote to Josephine from Tortona, June 15, 1796, and which at last induced her to join a husband who loved her madly. Perhaps there are traces here and there of Jean Jacques Rousseau's declamatory eloquence, but still in this volcanic style, emotion and truth and accents of sincere conviction are very manifest.

> "Tortona, Midday, the 27th Prairial, Year IV. of the
> Republic [June 15, 1796].

### "To Josephine.

"My life is a perpetual nightmare. A black presentiment makes breathing difficult. I am no longer alive; I have lost more than life, more than happi-

ness, more than peace; I am almost without hope.
I am sending you a courier. He will stay only four
hours in Paris, and then will bring me your answer.
Write to me ten pages; that is the only thing that
can console me in the least. You are ill; you love
me; I have distressed you; you are with child; and
I don't see you. This thought overwhelms me.
[Symptoms which amounted to nothing had in fact
delayed Josephine's departure for Italy, and her
husband reproached himself for having been unkind
to her.] I have treated you so ill that I do not
know how to set myself right in your eyes. I have
been blaming you for staying in Paris, and you have
been ill there. Forgive me, my dear; the love with
which you have filled me has robbed me of my
reason, and I shall never recover it. It is a malady
from which there is no recovery. My forebodings
are so gloomy that all I ask is to see you, to hold
you in my arms for two hours, and that we may die
together. Who is taking care of you? I suppose
that you have sent for Hortense; I love the dear
child a thousand times better since I think that she
may console you a little. As for me, I am without
consolation, rest, and hope until I see again the messenger whom I am sending to you, and until you
explain to me in a long letter just what is the matter
with you and how serious it is. If there were any
danger, I warn you that I should start at once for
Paris. . . . I have always been fortunate; never
has my fate opposed my wishes, and to-day I am

wounded when alone: I am sensitive. . . . With no appetite, unable to sleep, having lost all interest in friendship, in glory, in my country. You! you! and the rest of the world will not exist for me any more than if it had been annihilated. I care for honor, because you care for it, for victory, because it brings you pleasure: otherwise I should have abandoned everything to throw myself at your feet."

Walter Scott says, in his *Life of Napoleon:* "A part of his correspondence with his bride has been preserved, and gives a curious picture of a temperament as fiery in love as in war. The language of the conqueror, who was disposing states at his pleasure and defeating the most celebrated commanders of his time, is as enthusiastic as that of an Arcadian."

The last lines of the letter we have quoted above certainly confirm the great novelist's remark: "My dear, do remember to tell me that you are certain that I love you more than can be imagined, that you are convinced that my every moment is devoted to you; that no hour passes that I do not think of you; that it has never entered my mind to think of any other woman; that to me they all lack grace, beauty, and intelligence; that you, you as I see you, as you are, can please me and absorb my whole soul; that you have wholly filled it; that my heart has no corners that you do not see, no thoughts that are not subordinate to you; that my strength, my arms, my intelligence, are all yours; that my soul is in your body; and that the day when you shall have changed or shall have ceased to live will be the day of my death ; that nature, the earth, is beautiful in my eyes only because you live on it. If you do not believe that, if your soul is not convinced, penetrated, you distress me, you do not love me. There is a magnetic fluid between two persons who are in love. You know that I could never endure to see you in love with any one, still less endure that you should have a lover; to tear out his heart and to see him would be one and the same thing, and then, if I could raise my hand against your sacred person — No ! I should never dare, but I should at once abandon a life in which the most virtuous being in the world had deceived me." This letter, in which his jealousy thus breaks forth, ends with an outburst of confidence and enthusiasm: " I am certain and proud of your love. Our misfortunes are trials which only strengthen the force of our passion. A child as lovely as its mamma will one day be born to you. Wretch that I am, I only ask one day. A thousand kisses on your eyes, your lips. Adorable woman, how great a power you have over me ! I am ill with thy complaint ! I have again a burning fever ! Don't delay the courier more than six hours, and let him return at once with the dear letter of my queen."

Josephine could not withstand this appeal. She was quite recovered, and she was to be installed in splendor at Milan. Nevertheless, according to one of her intimate friends, the poet Arnault, she felt very sad at leaving Paris. He speaks thus about this delicate matter in his curious and witty Memoirs : " Josephine was evidently flattered by the love with which she inspired so wonderful a man as Bonaparte, although she treated the matter much more lightly than he ; she was proud to see that he loved her as much as he loved glory ; she enjoyed this glory, which was growing every day, but she preferred enjoying it in Paris, amid the applause which always followed her with every new bulletin from the Army of Italy. Her grief was extreme when she saw that she could no longer postpone her departure. She thought much more of what she was leaving than of what she was going to find, and she would have given the palace at Milan that was made ready for her, — she would have given all the palaces in the world for her house in the rue Chantereine, for the little house she had just bought of Talma. . . . It was from the Luxembourg that she started for Italy, after supping there with some of her friends, of whom I was one. . . . Poor woman ! she burst into tears, and sobbed as if she were going to her execution : she was going to reign."

The passport which the Directory gave to Madame Bonaparte bore the date of June 24, 1796. A few days afterwards she reached Milan, entering the city in a carriage in which were her brother-in-law Joseph, Junot, her husband's aide-de-camp, and a young officer named Hippolyte Charles, a captain on the staff of Adjutant-General Leclerc. The Duke of Serbelloni, who had gone to meet her at the gates of the city, followed in a second carriage. Unfortunately, when she arrived, Bonaparte was away on some military duty, and it was not for several days that he had the pleasure of seeing her. Marmont, who had been sent on ahead of Josephine, and had seen the numerous attentions paid to her by the Sardinian court, as she passed through Piedmont, says of the meeting of the happy couple : " Once at Milan, General Bonaparte was very happy, for then he lived only for his wife; for a long time this had been the case : never did a purer, truer, or more exclusive love fill a man's heart, or the heart of so extraordinary a man."

# V.

BONAPARTE'S condition had been greatly changed since he had parted from Josephine, and she must have been greatly surprised at seeing the position he occupied. Great results had been obtained, and he wore an air of victorious superiority, such as belonged to but few kings or princes. The archduke who had ruled over Lombardy a few weeks earlier had been far from possessing such authority. Bonaparte did not occupy the archduke's palace, lest he should offend the republican susceptibilities of the Directory; but he had a truly princely residence, the palace of a great and noble patriot of Milan, the Duke of Serbelloni. He had just been negotiating as an equal with the King of Sardinia, the Pope, the Duke of Modena, and the Grand Duke of Tuscany. Venice and Genoa had just been overcome by force and political manœuvring; Rome and Naples had been detached from the coalition; Upper Italy freed from the Austrian yoke; the most wonderful masterpieces of antiquity had been sent to Paris as part of the booty of the campaign: these were the marvels wrought in a very few days.

From the Alps to the Apennines, from the mountains of Tyrol to Vesuvius, the whole peninsula resounded with the name of Bonaparte. But he had to sustain this brilliant rôle, and preserve the glory he had so swiftly acquired. Austria was raising armies much superior in numbers to the force they were to meet. The Pope and the Neapolitan court were most ardently devoted to the success of the Austrians. At the first reverse of the young conqueror this framework of power which he had built up so gloriously would fall to the ground like a card house. Liberal ideas were then only on the surface in Italy; below them ruled the spirit of reaction. He could not count on Venice, where the old aristocracy was full of uneasiness; nor on the King of Sardinia, who yearned for revenge; nor on the King of Naples, whose wife was the sister of Queen Marie Antoinette; nor on the Grand Duke of Tuscany, who was an Austrian Archduke; nor on the Republic of Genoa, with its oligarchy in the pay of England; nor on the Pope, who looked only with horror on an army of Jacobins. In short, everything had to be done over again; and no sooner had he had the joy of seeing his wife than he was compelled to leave her again for the wars. His love was so impetuous that he even determined to take Josephine with him. This was an unheard-of innovation; but Bonaparte was not accustomed to imitating others: he did only what seemed good to him.

He left Milan to try to capture Mantua before the

arrival of the army commanded by Wurmser, and, July 6, 1796, wrote from Roverbella to Josephine, who had stayed in Milan: "I have beaten the enemy; Kilmaine will send you a copy of my report. I am dead tired. I beg of you to go at once to Verona: I need you, for I believe I am going to be ill. I send you a thousand kisses. I am in bed." July 11, there is another letter, from Verona: "I had hardly left Roverbella when I learned that the enemy was appearing before Verona. Masséna made the preparations, which turned out most fortunately. We have taken six hundred prisoners and captured their cannon. General Brune had seven bullets through his clothes, but not a scratch: that's good luck. I send you a thousand kisses. I am very well. We had only ten killed and a hundred wounded." July 17, Bonaparte wrote from Marmirolo to Josephine a letter worthy of the most ardent lover: "I have received your letter, my dear one, and it fills my heart with joy. I am very grateful to you for your trouble in sending me word about yourself: you ought to be better to-day. I am sure that you must be quite well. I beg of you to ride on horseback; it can't fail to do you good. Since I left you I have been continually sad. My only happiness is to be with you. I am continually recalling your kisses, your tears, your kind jealousy, and the fair Josephine's charms are forever kindling a blazing fire in my heart and my senses. When, free from all uneasiness and all business, shall I be able to pass all my time with you, to have nothing to do but to love you, and to think of nothing but of the happiness of telling and proving it to you? I will send you your horse, but I hope that you will soon be able to join me."

The letter concludes with an outburst of enthusiastic passion: "A few days ago I thought I loved you; but since I have seen you I feel that I love you a thousand times more. Since I have known you, I adore you every day more: this proves that what La Bruyère says about love coming in a flash, is false. Everything in nature has its course and different stages of growth. Ah! I beg of you let me see some of your faults! Be less beautiful, less graceful, less tender, less kind; above all, be never jealous, never weep: your tears rob me of my reason; they fire my blood. Be sure that it is not in my power to have a thought which is not yours or an idea which does not refer to you. Rest well; be strong soon. Come to me and let us at least be able to say before we die, So many days we were happy! Millions of kisses, and even to Fortuné, in spite of his crossness." Fortuné was Josephine's lap-dog.

July 18, there was another letter, also written at Marmirolo: "I have spent the whole night under arms. I should have taken Mantua by a bold and lucky blow, had not the water of the lake fallen so rapidly that my column, which had embarked, could not get there. This evening I am going to try again, a different plan. . . . I have a letter from Eugene, which I enclose. I beg of you to write for me to the dear children, and to send them some trinkets. Tell them that I love them as if they were my own children. Yours and mine are so mingled in my heart that there is no difference. I am very anxious to know how you are and what you are doing. I have been to Virgil's village, on the banks of the lake, in the silvery light of the moon, and there was not a moment when I did not think of Josephine."

Michelet, in his volume entitled *Until the 18th Brumaire*, comments as follows on this sentence: "In the course of the siege of Mantua, Bonaparte said to Josephine in a sentimental letter, which bears all the marks of the taste of the time, that while thinking of her, in melancholy revery, he had visited Virgil's village on the lake in the moonlight. It was doubtless then that he conceived the notion of the festival in honor of the great poet, which he ordered later, and which was of great service to him with society, nurtured in worship of the classics. In engravings we often see the hero of Italy near Virgil's tomb and under the shadow of his laurel."

Whatever may be said, there was a tender and sentimental chord in Napoleon's character. "Nature had given him," says the Duke of Ragusa in his Memoirs, "a grateful and kindly, I might almost say sensitive, heart. This assertion will contradict many fixed but inaccurate opinions. His sensitiveness evaporated in time, but in the course of my writing I shall narrate incidents and give undeniable proofs of the accuracy of my opinion." Napoleon was fond of poetry. It was he who said at Saint Helena, "Imagination rules the world." In literature, nothing ever seemed to him high enough, ideal enough. His whole childhood was passed in ardent meditation upon the poets and great men. He was equally interested in Homer and Alexander, in Virgil and Cæsar. As a student of Plutarch and Jean Jacques Rousseau, he belonged to the idealist school, and he admired everything great, everything beautiful. He loved love as he loved glory; that is to say, without bounds. The style of his proclamations and bulletins harmonizes with that of his love-letters. As hero or as lover, he is always the same man.

Bonaparte wrote again from Marmirolo, July 19: "I have not heard from you for two days; I have said this same thing thirty times to-day; you will see that this is very gloomy; nevertheless, you cannot doubt of the tender and single interest you inspire me with. Yesterday we attacked Mantua. We set it on fire with two batteries firing red-hot balls and shells. The unhappy city burned all night. It was a horrible and impressive sight. We have got possession of many of the outlying works, and open our trenches to-night. I am to transfer headquarters to Castiglione to-morrow, and I mean to sleep there. I have received a courier from Paris. There were two letters for you; I have read them. Nevertheless, although this act seems to me perfectly simple, and you gave me free leave the other day, I fear that you may be annoyed, and this thought distresses me much. I should have liked to seal them again. Fie! that would have been disgraceful. If I am to blame, I beg your pardon; I give you my word that I was not moved by jealousy: no, certainly, I respect my dear one too much for that. I wish you would give me absolute permission to read your letters; then I should suffer from neither remorse nor fear. Achille has come with despatches from Milan; no letters from my dear one! Farewell, my only love! When can we meet? I shall come to Milan myself to get you. A thousand kisses, as warm as my heart, as pure as you are. I have had the courier summoned: he tells me that he called on you, and that you said you had nothing for him. Shame! wicked, ugly, cruel tyrant; pretty little monster! You laugh at my threats, at my foolishness; ah, if I only could put you in my heart, you know I should lock you up there! Tell me that you are happy, well, and very loving."

From Castiglione, Bonaparte wrote to Josephine, July 21: "I hope that I shall find a letter from you when I arrive this evening. You know, dear Josephine, what pleasure your letters give me; and I am sure you like to write them. I leave, this evening, for Peschiera and Verona; then I shall go to Mantua, and possibly to Milan, to get a kiss, since you assure me they are not of ice. I hope to find you perfectly recovered, and that you will be able to go to headquarters with me, and not to leave me again. Are you not the soul of my life and the passion of my heart? Good by, lovely and kind creature, without a rival, you dear goddess; a thousand loving kisses!"

But Wurmser was advancing. Bonaparte could not go to Milan for Josephine; but he persuaded her to join him, by means of this letter from Castiglione, July 22: "The army requires my presence here; it is quite impossible for me to go so far away as Milan. That would take five or six days; and in that time something might happen which would make my presence indispensable. You tell me you are perfectly well; then, I beg of you to come to Brescia. I am sending Murat to prepare a lodging for you there, such as you want. I think you would do well to rest on the 6th [Thermidor], and to leave Milan very late, reaching Brescia on the 7th, where the most devoted of lovers will be awaiting you. I am sorry that you can imagine, my dear one, that my heart has room for any one besides you: it belongs to you by right of conquest, and this conquest will be solid and eternal. I don't know why you mention Madame T., in whom I take very little interest, as in the women of Brescia. As to those letters which you are sorry I opened, this one shall be the last; your letter had not reached me. Good by, my dear; let me hear from you often. Come speedily to me; be happy and perfectly easy: all is going on well, and my heart is yours for life. Don't fail to return to Adjutant-General Miollis the box of medals that he wrote to me he had given to you.

Mankind is so malicious and gossiping that one cannot be too careful.   Be well, love me, and come soon to Brescia.   At Milan, I have a carriage for both town and country use: you will use that for your journey. Bring what silverware you need, and whatever may be necessary.   Travel slowly, and in the cool of the day, to avoid getting tired.   It takes the soldiers only three days to go to Brescia.   You can post for fourteen hours of the way.   I advise you to sleep, the 6th, at Cassano: I will go as far as I can to meet you, on the 7th.   Good by, dear Josephine! a thousand loving kisses."

By thus calling his wife to him, in time of war, between two battles, Bonaparte seemed to be doing something very rash; yet — for at that time he was always successful — he perhaps owed his safety to this apparently unjustifiable resolution.   Josephine seemed his good angel.   We may say that throughout his career, so long as he was with her, he always enjoyed the most brilliant success.   A gambler — and politics is a game, like almost all other human things — would say that she brought him good luck.

Josephine did not fail to meet him at Brescia, as he had appointed; but scarcely had they got there when, July 28, they had to leave.   Wurmser had received word of the critical condition of Mantua, and had hastened his march some eight or ten days, which compelled the French army to hasten in its turn.   General de Ségur says in his Memoirs: " To picture the disorder, the urgent peril into which

Wurmser's double attack at first threw Bonaparte, let us listen to Josephine herself, who used to take pleasure in telling us how, when the movement began, she was quietly in Brescia, and the *provedi- tore* was trying to tempt her to stay one night longer, by proposing a grand entertainment. It was she, she told me, who refused so obstinately that she per- suaded Bonaparte to leave at once. This happy inspiration saved them. They were not four leagues from Brescia when the Austrians, in league with the *proveditore*, entered in large force. Bonaparte would have been captured at the ball, and either put to death or made prisoner of war."

The next day Josephine was of no less service to her husband. At dawn the two reached a castle close to Verona, escorted by twenty men at the most; there they were assailed by other forces of the enemy who had come down the Adige. Josephine's eyes, which were better than her husband's, had given her notice of this new danger, and he fancied that he saved her from it by sending her to the shores of Lake Garda. But there, on the other hand, she was greeted by new bullets from a hostile flotilla which controlled the lake. Abandoning her carriage, she mounted a horse and fled to Peschiera, where Bonaparte, who had received word, sent for her. She rejoined him at Castiglione. At every step she came across soldiers wounded in the skirmishes pre- ceding the great battles.

Bonaparte, seeing her in such peril, decided to

make her return to Brescia; but Josephine was stopped by a division of the enemy which had already reached Ponte Marco on its way towards Lonato. She was obliged to retrace her steps and to return to Castiglione, where Bonaparte still was. " At that time," says the *Memorial of Saint Helena*, " in the anxiety and excitement of the moment, she was frightened and wept much." When Bonaparte heard that the Austrians had entered Brescia and that his communications with Milan were cut off, he sent his wife to Central Italy, making her pass before Mantua, which was still besieged by the French. Moved by the sorrow she showed in parting from him, he said, " Wurmser will have to pay dear for the tears he has caused you."

Since his marriage Bonaparte had passed but very few days with Josephine, and his love for her produced a certain excitement which made him ready to do great things. His wife's tears moved him deeply. " I shall console her," he said to himself, " she shall have every joy and glory. To that face now wet with tears I shall bring the glow of happiness." The climate of Italy, the bright sun, the clear sky, the summer heat, the excitement of war, the smell of powder, the fierceness of the conflict, the ardor of youth, all combined to fire the vivid imagination of the hero. He has reached one of those periods in the careers of great men, when they feel themselves lifted above the earth by a supernatural breath, and they are moved by a mysterious force, as if they

were divinely inspired. Men of action and artists
know those privileged moments when they become
capable of wonders. With the character that he
possessed, Bonaparte could not appear before Josephine as a beaten man. He wanted to dazzle, to
fascinate her, to wring from her cries of admiration,
to cover her with glory. If he had been beaten, he
would have scorned all pity and consolation. His
patriotism and his love fired him with the determination to triumph. His nature, already compact of
energy, renewed its strength and audacity, and he
was irresistible. It was when he saw Josephine in
tears that love, ambition, pride, and hunger for
victory took possession of his soul and gave to his
genius a fire, an impulse, a development, such as it is
hard to conceive. He said: "I shall see her again,
and it will be when I shall have triumphed." Hence
he had to conquer at any price. He wished victory
for the sake of France and for the sake of Josephine.
That day he had no mistrust of fortune ; he believed
in his lucky star more firmly than ever. A secret
voice said to him, "Forward!" Josephine herself
must have been reassured by her husband's eagle
glance. The six days' campaign was about to open.
A woman's love was the talisman with which Bonaparte was about to work miracles.

Nevertheless, Josephine was in flight, passing in
her carriage very near to besieged Mantua. She was
fired on from the town, and some of her escort were
hit. General de Ségur narrates what she herself told

him that, as they were passing by within gunshot, the firing was so hot that she was obliged to take refuge in a chapel. A soldier ran up to urge them to leave, showing them some Austrian cannon aimed at that dangerous place. In fact, she had scarcely got away before the cannon-balls destroyed the building. She crossed the Po, and reached Lucca, going through Bologna and Ferrara, "pursued," says the *Memorial of Saint Helena*, "by fear and all the evil rumors which generally accompanied our armies, yet supported by her confidence in her husband's star. Already such was the state of public opinion in Italy and such the feeling inspired by the French general, that, in spite of the dangers of the moment and all the false rumors that were current, his wife was received at Lucca by the Senate and treated like a great princess: it went to congratulate her and presented her with gifts of precious oils. It was justified in these rejoicings, for a few days later messages announced her husband's wonderful successes and the total defeat of Wurmser." Just when she had crossed the Po, and put that river between herself and Wurmser's uhlans, Josephine received a letter from Bonaparte, dated August 4, in which, discounting the future, he announced to her, as already won, the victory of the next day.

# VI.

BETWEEN CASTIGLIONE AND ARCOLE.

A T Wurmser's approach, Bonaparte exclaimed, "We are now to watch each other; bad luck to him who makes a mistake!" Bonaparte made no mistake. His army consisted of only forty-two thousand men; that of his adversary, of sixty thousand. The foes of France uttered cries of joy. At Venice, the soldiers thronged the public places and held out their hands to the passers-by, asking for the price of the French blood which they were about to shed. At Rome, the French agents were insulted. The court of Naples broke the armistice. Italy was called the grave of the French. On hearing that the Austrians were about to cross the Adige at every point, that retreat on Milan was cut off, that the position at Rivoli was to be forced as well as at Corona, Bonaparte, July 3, called a council of war. The generals favored a retreat. Augereau alone held out for fighting: this was also Bonaparte's opinion.

The town of Castiglione, which lies ten leagues to the northeast of Mantua, and three leagues south of Lonato, is within reach of two Tyrolese

passes, — that of the Adige, to the eastward of
Lake Garda, and that of the west shore of this
lake. Although the enemy had forced the line of
the Adige, the position was so favorable that it presented many advantages to a man of Bonaparte's
audacious genius. Raising the siege of Mantua,
because he knew that in moments of great peril, to
try to save everything is the sure way to lose everything, he concentrated all his forces at the end of
the lake. Then, pursuing his usual tactics, he, by
his swift movements, doubled his strength, and
wherever he gave battle it was with equal or superior force. Successful at Lonato, August 3d, and on
the 5th at Castiglione, he wrote on the 8th to the
Directory that the Austrian army had vanished like
a dream and that Italy was tranquil. Wurmser had
just withdrawn, leaving ninety cannon, and twenty-
five thousand picked men killed or captured. August
9, Bonaparte wrote a letter thanking the city of
Milan for remaining faithful to him: " The ardor and
the character which the city has displayed," he said,
"have won the esteem and the love of France; its
population, which is ever becoming more energetic,
becomes every day more worthy to be free: some
day, without doubt, it will enter on the stage of the
world with glory." Marmont wrote to his father:
"In the last week I have not slept four hours.
There are none of the enemy left for us to fight
with, and we are going, I hope, to enjoy our triumphs."

Bonaparte, who had returned to Brescia August 10,

wrote that same evening to Josephine, who, after the victory at Castiglione, had been able to return to Milan without difficulty. "I have just arrived, and my first thought is to write to you. All the way I have been thinking of nothing but your health and your image. I shall not be easy till I have heard from you. I am waiting impatiently; I can't express my uneasiness. I left you sad, depressed, and half ill. If the sincerest and tenderest love can make you happy, you must be so. . . . I am up to my ears in work. Good by, my sweet Josephine; love me well, keep well, and think of me often."

After renewing the siege of Mantua, Bonaparte went to Milan, where he spent a fortnight with his wife. Wurmser, who had fled to the Tyrol, wanted to resume the offensive; and Austria was about to raise a new army, that of Alvinzy. Bonaparte had to begin the campaign once more. He left Josephine at Milan, and started again for the war with that untiring zeal which was the amazement and the despair of his enemies. All these preoccupations, dangers, and battles could not distract him from his love, which was continually growing in intensity. It was a perpetual fever. When he had reached Brescia, he wrote to Josephine, August 31: "I leave at once for Verona. I had hopes of finding a letter from you; this leaves me in horrible anxiety. You were not very well before I left; I beg of you, don't leave me in such anxiety. You had promised to be more thoughtful; yet your words then agreed with your heart. . . . You, to whom nature has given sweetness, gentleness, and every attractive quality, how can you forget one who loves you so warmly? Three days without a word from you, and I have written to you several times. This absence is horrible; the nights are long, tiresome, dull; the days are monotonous. To-day, alone with my thoughts, my work, my writing, with men and their tedious plans, I have not even one note from you to press against my heart. Headquarters have gone on; I follow in an hour. I have received an express from Paris this evening; there was nothing for you but the enclosed letter, which will give you pleasure. Think of me; live for me; be often with your loving one; and believe that the only misfortune he dreads is to be loved no longer by Josephine. A thousand gentle, loving, exclusive kisses!'"

Another letter, from Ala, September 3, 1796: "We are in the midst of the campaign, my dear one; we have overthrown the enemy's posts and have captured eight or ten horses with as many men. I hope that we shall have good luck, and enter Trent the 19th [Fructidor]. No letters from you, and this makes me really uneasy; still I hear that you are well, and that you have even been out sailing on Lake Como. I am impatiently expecting every day the courier with word from you; you know how much I want to hear from you. I do not really live, away from you; my life's happiness is only to be with my sweet Josephine. Think of me! write to me often, very often : it is the only balm in absence, which is cruel, but I hope will be short."

Bonaparte's soldiers rivalled the Alpine hunters in boldness and activity : they clambered over the rocks to the mountain tops, and thence sent a plunging fire upon the enemy below. The swiftness of their heroic deeds was most remarkable. September 4, the victory of Roveredo ; the 5th, entrance into Trent ; the pursuit of Wurmser in the gorges of the Brenta ; the seizure of the defile of Primolano ; September 8th, the victory of Bassano. Two hours later, the successful general wrote to the Directory : "In six days we have fought two battles and four skirmishes ; we have taken twenty-one flags from the enemy ; made sixteen thousand prisoners, including several generals ; the rest have been killed, wounded, or scattered to the four winds. In these six days, continually fighting in inexpugnable gorges, we have made forty-five leagues, captured seventy cannon with their caissons and horses, a great part of the ammunition, and large stores."

September 10, Bonaparte wrote from Montebello to his wife : "My dear, the enemy has had eighteen thousand men taken prisoner : the rest are killed or wounded. Wurmser, with a column of five hundred horse and five thousand men, has no resource but to throw himself into Mantua. Never have we had such constant and important success. Italy, Trieste, and the Tyrol are secured for the Republic. The Emperor will have to raise a second army ; artillery, pontoons, baggage, everything has been captured. In a few days we shall meet; that is the sweetest reward of my fatigue and my cares. A thousand ardent and loving kisses."

While Bonaparte was winning these astounding victories, what was Josephine's state of mind at Milan? To tell the truth, Josephine was bored. M. Aubenas has published a letter which she wrote at this time to her aunt, Madame de Renaudin, who had just married the Marquis of Beauharnais. This letter, which has been preserved among the papers of the Tascher de la Pagerie family, betrays the melancholy which came over Josephine in her separation from her children and her Paris friends. The Duke of Serbelloni who was going to Paris, was the bearer of this letter, which ran thus: " M. Serbelloni will tell you, my dear aunt, how I have been received in Italy, *fêted* everywhere, all the Italian princes giving me entertainments, even the Grand Duke of Tuscany, the Emperor's brother. Well! I had rather be a simple private person in France. I don't like the honors of this country. I am frightfully bored. It is true that the state of my health has something to do with my low spirits; I am often ailing. If happiness could make me well, I ought to be in the very best health; I have the best husband that can be imagined. I have no chance to want anything. My wishes are his. He adores me all day long, as if I were a goddess; there cannot be a better husband. M. Serbelloni will tell you how much I am loved. He often writes to my

HORTENSE BEAUHARNAIS

QUEEN OF HOLLAND

children; he loves them much. He sends to Hortense, by M. Serbelloni a handsome watch, a repeater, enamelled and set in small pearls; to Eugene, a fine gold watch. . . . Good by, my dear aunt, my dear mamma; do not forget how much I love you. I shall try to send you a little money for the purpose you mentioned at the first opportunity."

At the same time Josephine wrote to her daughter Hortense from Milan, September 6, 1796, as follows: " The Duke of Serbelloni is leaving for Paris, and has promised to go to Saint Germain, my dear Hortense, the day after his arrival. He will tell you how much I think and speak of and how much I love you! Eugene also partakes of these feelings, my dear girl; I love you both very dearly. M. Serbelloni will bring you from Bonaparte and me some little souvenirs for you, Emilie, Eugene, and Jerome. Give my love to Madame Campan; I am going to send her some fine engravings and drawings from Italy. Kiss my dear Eugene, Emilie, and Jerome for me. Good by, my dear Hortense, my dear girl. Think often of your mamma; write to her often; your letters and your brother's will console me for my absence from my dear children; I kiss you affectionately."

The untiring Bonaparte continued his victorious course. September 15, he compelled Wurmser to take refuge in Mantua. But amid all his successes, he was unhappy because Josephine's letters were too rare. He wrote to her, September 17, from Verona, this melancholy epistle: " I write to you very often, and you write very seldom. You are a wicked, ugly woman, as ugly as you are frivolous. It is a bit of perfidy to deceive a husband, a doting lover, in this way! Must he lose all his rights because he is away, overwhelmed with work, fatigue, and trouble? How can he help it? Yesterday we had a very hot fight; the enemy lost heavily and was thoroughly beaten. We captured the suburb of Mantua. Good by, dear Josephine. One of these nights your door will be burst open, as if a jealous husband were breaking in, and I shall be in your arms. A thousand loving kisses."

A letter from Modena, October 17, is likewise filled with sadness. " Day before yesterday I was in the field all day. Yesterday I stayed in bed. A fever and a raging headache prevented me from writing to my dear one; but I received her letters. I pressed them to my heart and my lips; and the pang of absence, a hundred miles apart, vanished. At that moment, I saw you with me, — not capricious and vexed, but gentle, loving, with that grace of kindness which belongs to Josephine alone. It was a dream; judge for yourself whether it relieved my fever. Your letters are as cold as fifty years of age; one would think they had been written after we had been married fifteen years. They are full of the friendliness and feelings of life's winter. Shame! Josephine. It is very wicked, very bad, very traitorous of you. What more can you do to distress me? Stop loving me? That you have already done. Hate me? Well, I wish you would: everything degrades me except hatred; but indifference with a calm pulse, fixed eyes, monotonous walk! . . . A thousand kisses, tender, like my heart. I am a little better, and shall leave to-morrow. The English are evacuating the Mediterranean. Corsica is ours. Good news for France and for the army!"

Between Wurmser's entrance into Mantua, September 18, and Alvinzy's arrival on the Brenta and the Adige, early in November, there was a respite in the military movements of about five or six weeks. During this time Bonaparte was opposing the policy of the Directory, which was hostile to his views, and failed to send him the necessary re-enforcements. The troops who had been often promised failed to arrive. There was no money to pay the soldiers. The Army of Italy was reduced to thirty-three thousand men: and it was with this insufficient force that he was expected to retake Corsica; control the whole peninsula; besiege twenty-two thousand Austrians who had taken refuge in Mantua; intimidate the Roman and Neapolitan courts, which were driven to extremities by the unreasonable demands of the Directory; and, in addition, oppose the new and formidable Austrian force under the command of Alvinzy.

Bonaparte became impatient. October 6, he wrote to the Directory: "Everything in Italy is going to ruin. The glory of our forces is fading away. Our numbers are counted. The influence of Rome is

incalculable. It was very unwise to break with that
power. If I had been consulted on all that, I should
have continued negotiations with Rome, as with
Genoa and Venice. Whenever your general in Italy
is not the centre of everything, you will run great
risks. This language must not be ascribed to ambition ; I have all the honors I want, and my health is
so shattered that I fancy I shall have to ask to have
some one put in my place." Was this demand sincere, or a feint? And would Bonaparte have been
pained if the Directory had taken him at his word?
However this may be, he had already written to
Carnot, August 9: "If there is in France a single
man, honest and true, who can suspect my political
intentions, I at once resign the pleasure of serving
my country. Three or four months of retirement
will silence envy, restore my health, and enable me
to fill to better advantage whatever position the
government may entrust to me. When the time
shall have come, it will only be by leaving the Army
of Italy in season, that I shall be able to devote the
rest of my life to the defence of the Republic. Not
to let men grow old is the whole art of government.
When I entered a public career, I adopted for my
principle : Everything for my country ! I beg of
you to believe in the feelings of esteem and friendship which I have avowed to you."

When Alvinzy was advancing with an army of
apparently overwhelming force, and nothing short
of a miracle could save the French troops, the young

commander-in-chief, who, for the first time perhaps, doubted of his star, possibly regretted that the
Directory had not accepted his resignation. But the
lot was thrown! he had to try the impossible. Bonaparte was a man of dauntless audacity. He did not
lose heart; his genius grew with the danger.

# VII.

## ARCOLE.

AFTER a successful war it appears as if the victor had known no other feeling than joy, enthusiasm, and confidence. The mere name of the first Italian campaign calls up visions of zeal and triumph, and yet it was full of uncertainty and anxiety. Often everything seemed lost; often Bonaparte escaped as if by a miracle. The hostile armies, which appeared one after another; the perpetual dwindling of the heroic brigades; the illness which continually afflicted the young commander-in-chief and filled him with despondency, — all that is forgotten before the glory of the results obtained, before the brilliancy of the victory. But Bonaparte's soul was torn by ceaseless anxiety. What would be his place in history? Would he be called foolhardy or a hero? This depended on his success. And on what did his success depend? If he were beaten, all the old-fashioned tacticians would turn him to ridicule and prove by mathematical reasoning that his plans were all wild visions, and that defeat was inevitable because he knew nothing of the art of war. In order to justify his self-confidence, he had to beat. His future depended on the numberless accidents which decide the issue of battles. At every moment of this memorable campaign he was on the edge of a precipice. A touch, and he was over. It is when we study the lives of the greatest men, the Cæsars, the Alexanders, the Napoleons, that we are most impressed with the insignificance of human affairs and the very great importance of the most insignificant details of the most trivial incidents in the fate of republics and empires. There is an unknown force which mocks all human plans. The faithful call it Providence ; sceptics call it chance. But whatever its name, it exists everywhere. Almost all great geniuses are fatalists, because, when they examine their own triumphs, they see how small was their own part, and that often they have failed when, according to every reasonable view, they should have succeeded, and have succeeded when success was hopeless. But of these things public opinion takes no account. It cares for but one thing, — success ; and its favorites are those who have risked everything for everything, and won.

When Alvinzy's army was advancing towards the Piave, Bonaparte had but thirty-six thousand men to oppose to sixty thousand, and they were exhausted by three campaigns and by the fevers which they caught in the rice-fields of Lombardy. Any one else would have despaired. November 5, he wrote to the Directory : " Everything suffers, and we are in face of the enemy ! The least delay may be fatal to us. We are on the

eve of great events.   These delays are a terrible misfortune for us.   All the troops of the Empire have
reached their posts with surprising celerity, and we
are left to ourselves.   Fine promises and a few insignificant corps are all that we have received."

After a few successes of the outposts, followed by
several serious reverses, Bonaparte had been forced
to a double retreat.   His left wing, under the command of Vaubois, had occupied Trent; it was driven
back on Corona and Rivoli.   He himself, with seventeen thousand men, had taken position before Verona,
on the Brenta.   He had been driven back into Verona,
whence he wrote this brief letter to Josephine, November 9: "I reached Verona day before yesterday.
Though I am tired, I am very well, very busy, always
passionately devoted to you.   My horse is waiting.
A thousand kisses."   November 11, he attacked
Alvinzy again, but again he failed.   The two divisions of Augereau and Masséna tried, November 12,
to capture the heights of Caldiero.   The unfavorable
weather, the numerical superiority of the enemy, the
strength of their positions, all contributed to the ill-
success of these two divisions, in spite of all their
heroism.   They were repulsed, and they withdrew
into Verona.   Then, perhaps for the first time, the
valiant Army of Italy felt discouraged.   Vaubois
had not more than six thousand men.   There were
not more than thirteen thousand in Masséna's and
Augereau's divisions together.

The soldiers sadly said: "We can't alone do the

work of all. Alvinzy's army, which faces us, is the
one before which the armies of the Rhine and of
the Sambre-et-Meuse retreated, and they are idle
now: why should we have to do their work? They
don't send us any re-enforcements; if we are beaten,
we shall flee to the Alps, disgraced. If, on the other
hand, we are victorious, of what use will the new
victory be? We shall be confronted with a new
army like Alvinzy's, just as Alvinzy has succeeded
Wurmser, and in this unceasing and unequal struggle
we must be ruined in the end."

The enemy were able to count the reduced forces
of the French at their leisure. They felt confident of
victory, and were already preparing the ladders with
which they meant to scale the walls of Verona. Bonaparte's situation seemed desperate. Yet at this critical moment, on the day after his defeat at Caldiero,
November 13, he found time to write an affectionate
and reproachful letter to Josephine: "I don't love
you at all; in fact, I hate you. You are horrid,
clumsy, stupid, a perfect Cinderella. You never
write to me; you don't love your husband the least
bit in the world; you know what pleasure your letters give him, and you won't send him six lines!
What do you do all day? What is there serious
enough to keep you from writing to your dear lover?
What affection kills and throws to one side the love,
the tender and constant love, which you promised him?
Who is this wonderful creature, this new lover, who
takes all your time, rules all your days, and prevents

your writing to your husband? Josephine, take care; some fine night your door shall be burst open, and there I am. Seriously, I am uneasy, my dear, at not hearing from you. Write me four pages at once, and all sorts of loving things which will fill my heart with love and emotion. I hope soon to hold you in my arms, and I shall cover you with a million kisses as hot as the equator."

Madame de Rémusat, always disposed to deny Bonaparte any trace of feeling, and ready to maintain that he was all intelligence, was, in spite of herself, struck by the passion which fills this correspondence. She says in her Memoirs: "I have seen some of Napoleon's letters to his wife written in the first Italian campaign. . . . These letters are very singular; they are in an almost undecipherable handwriting, they are badly spelt, the style is strange and confused. Yet they have such a passionate tone, they are so full of real feeling, they contain expressions so warm, and at the same time so poetical, that there never lived a woman who would not have been glad to receive just such letters. They form a striking contrast with the delicate and measured smoothness of the letters of M. de Beauharnais. Moreover, what a thing for a woman to see herself — at a time when men were controlled by politics — one of the inspiring causes of an army's triumphal march! On the eve of one of his great battles, Bonaparte wrote: 'Here I am, far away from you! I seem to have fallen into the darkest shadows; I need the fatal fire of the thunderbolts which we are about to hurl on the enemy, to escape from the darkness into which your absence has cast me.'"

Nevertheless the danger grew to be very serious. Some years later, Josephine told General de Ségur, at Saint Cloud, that shortly before the battle of Arcole she had received a letter from Bonaparte in which he confessed that he had lost all hope, that everything was lost, and that everywhere the enemy was showing a force three times as large as his own; that nothing was left him but his courage; that probably he should lose the Adige; that then he should fight for the Mincio; and that this last position lost, he should, if alive, join Josephine at Genoa, whither he advised her to go.

Foreseeing the disorder, the bloodshed even, of which her departure from Milan would be the signal, Josephine decided to stay there, and she continued her usual life, with no change in her habits, going to the theatre with death in her heart, but presenting a calm front, in spite of the threatening air of a part of the populace of Milan. For three nights Italians went frequently even into her bedroom, waking her up, under the pretext of asking for news, but evidently in expectation of her departure, in order that their revolt might not be delayed a moment.

Before his men, Bonaparte assumed an air of perfect confidence. Even when his soul was torn by the cruelest distress and anxiety, his face remained impassible. At the very moment when he was promising his soldiers an early victory, he was writing to the Directory, November 14, an almost despairing letter: " Citizens Directors, I owe you an account of the operations which have taken place. If it is not satisfactory, you will not ascribe the fault to the army: its present inferiority and the exhaustion of its bravest men makes me dread the worst. It may be that we are about to lose all Italy! None of the expected aid has reached us. . . . I am doing my duty, and the same thing is true of the army. My soul is tortured, but my conscience is easy. . . . To-day, 24th Brumaire, the troops are resting. To-morrow our movements depend on the enemy. I have no hope of preventing the raising of the siege of Mantua, which was ours, in a week. If this blow falls, we shall soon be behind the Adda, and further still, if no troops arrive. . . . The Army of Italy, which is reduced to a mere handful, is exhausted. The heroes of Lodi, Millesimo, Castiglione, and Bassano have either died for their country or are in the hospital. There is nothing left but their reputation and their pride. Joubert, Lannes, Lannusse, Murat, Dupuis, Rambau, Chabran, are wounded. . . . The few who are left see death inevitable, amid such unending combats and with such inferior forces! Possibly the hour of the brave Augereau, of the fearless Masséna, of Berthier, is close at hand! Then* what will become of all these brave men? This idea disturbs me. I no longer dare to face death, which would bring discouragement and mis-

ery to all over whom I keep watch." The letter
begins in what is almost despair; it ends with hope-
fulness: "In a few days we shall make our final
effort! If fortune favors us, Mantua will be taken,
and with it Italy! Re-enforced by the army besieg-
ing that town, there is nothing I would not undertake!"

Everything seemed to point to Bonaparte's failure;
but a secret voice whispered to him, " You will be
saved!" There are men to whom difficulties are
but a stimulus, whom danger only makes bold. The
abyss causes them no giddiness, but only reassures
and encourages them. Before beginning the fight,
the young general thought that he saw Josephine's
image. Like the knights of old who evoked the
memory of their ladies before accomplishing their
exploits, he derived an irresistible strength from
the noble and chivalrous love that filled his heroic
and poetic soul. It was a curious spectacle — this
man amid the most engrossing occupations, yet hun-
gering for love, and in the moment of the most imminent peril consoling himself by expecting a kiss,
a smile! This impetuous genius, in the most terrible
crisis of his career, found time to be jealous, and to
suffer pangs of love! After promising his wife vast
power and endless glory, what would he not suffer
if his career were to be checked now at the start;
if all these hopes were to be but a disappointment; if
the pretended great man should appear as a mere
young braggart, unworthy of the confidence of a

Barras! What would then say his three mistresses, — Josephine, France, and Italy? To avoid such a disaster, he felt capable of prodigies. His genius, like his love, reached a pitch of wonderful intensity. Being anxious not to see Josephine till after a complete triumph, he remembered the line from the *Cid*, —

"Issue a victor from the combat of which Chimène is the prize!"

November 17, at nightfall, the camp at Verona was called to arms. At the news of the last reverses the sick and wounded insisted on leaving the hospital and taking their places in the ranks with their wounds yet unhealed; and their presence filled the army with lively emotion. The columns started, passed through Verona, and issued from the gate called the gate of Milan, and took a position on the right bank of the Adige. It was a solemn and anxious moment. They had no idea where they were going. The time of starting; the position they had taken on the right, and not on the left bank; the silence which was observed, while usually the order of the day announced an intended battle, — the whole state of affairs made them think that they were about to begin retreat. They feared that they were about to abandon Italy, that promised land, which they had won with so much glory, and to lose the fruit of such hot struggles and such dauntless courage. Were the heroes of so many battles to be fugitives? The mere thought filled them with dis-

tress; they yearned to continue the struggle as long
as they had a cartridge and a bayonet left. So when
instead of following the road to.Peschiera, the army
suddenly turned to the left, along the Adige, reaching
Ronco before daybreak, where it found Andréassy
there finishing the construction of a bridge, and dis-
covered itself by a simple turn to the left, on the other
bank of the Adige, there was general joy. "No!" exclaimed the soldiers, "we are not retreating. With
twelve thousand men we can do nothing in the open
country against forty-five thousand. Our general is
leading us to the causeways in the vast marshes, where
numbers will not count, but where everything will
depend on the courage of the heads of the columns.
Forward!" Then, as it is said in the *Memorial of
Saint Helena*, "the hope of victory fired every heart:
every man promised to outdo himself in support of
so fine and bold a plan." When Bonaparte saw the
glowing eyes of his soldiers before this battle of
giants, he felt that with such men he could hope
everything. There was about to begin a three days'
battle, one of the most stupendous struggles that an
army could ever undertake.

Three causeways run from Ronco, and all these
are surrounded by marshes. The first, ascending the
Adige, leads to Verona; the second, to Villa Nuova,
passing before Arcole, which has a bridge a league
and a half from the Adige, over the little river,
the Alpon; the third descends the Adige, towards
Albaredo. Three columns advanced simultaneously

over the three causeways. The centre column was marching on Arcole, and the skirmishers reached the bridge without being perceived by the enemy, who had been too careless to extend his outposts to the Adige, under the impression that the space between that river and the Alpon was an impassable marsh. The causeway from Ronco to Arcole strikes the Alpon at a distance of two miles, and from there runs up the right bank of the river for a mile and turns at right angles to the right, entering Arcole. Bonaparte reached this bridge which was to become so famous. He tried to cross it, but a terrible fire stopped the soldiers. Before this rain of bullets, this avalanche of cannon-balls and shells, even the boldest hesitated. Bonaparte galloped forward, and when near the bridge, got off his horse. Augereau's men had sought refuge in the marsh, and were crouching along the edge of the causeway to escape the storm of bullets that had repelled them. Their general shouted to them, " Are you no longer the men who conquered at Lodi?" and seizing a flag, he called to them and inspired them with his own courage. They followed him in spite of the deadly fire, and got within two hundred steps of the bridge, and were about to cross it, when a major seized Bonaparte by the waist, shouting, "General, you will be killed, and without you we are lost; you shall go no further!" Then they fell back. The soldiers, unwilling to abandon their general, seized his arm, his hair, his coat, and dragged him with them in their flight, amid the dead and dying, through the smoke. In the confusion, without seeing what they did, they threw him over to the right, into the marsh, and lost sight of him. The Austrians were there. Fortunately they failed to recognize him. A cry was heard, "Forward, men, to save the general!" Marmont, Louis Bonaparte, and a few other brave men rushed out, and tore the commander-in-chief from the thick mud into which he had fallen; they put him on his horse and charged the enemy, who at nightfall finally abandoned Arcole, retiring on San Bonifacio.

"That day," says the *Memorial of Saint Helena*, "was one of soldierly devotion. General Lannes had hastened from Milan; he had been wounded at Governolo, and was still weak. He placed himself between Napoleon and the enemy, covering him with his body, and was wounded in three places, insisting on not leaving him. Muiron, the general's aide-decamp, was killed while covering his general with his body, — a touching and heroic death."

The battle continued the next day, November 16, and the day after, the 17th. On the 16th, the Austrians were defeated on the dykes of the Adige and of Arcole. In the afternoon of the 17th, Bonaparte counted the losses of the enemy, and decided that it must have lost twenty thousand men, and that thus it was only one-third stronger than his own forces. Consequently, he ordered his troops to leave the marshes, and attack the Austrians on the plain. The army crossed the bridge that had been built at

the mouth of the Alpon. There was killed young Elliot, one of Bonaparte's aides-de-camp. At two in the
afternoon, the French were engaged, their left wing
at Arcole, their right in the direction of Porto
Lignano. The enemy was defeated at every point,
and, exhausted by a bloody contest of seventy-two
hours, they retreated in the direction of Vicenza.

November 18, Bonaparte, who had secretly marched
out from the Milan gate of Verona on the 14th,
re-entered the town in triumph, by the left bank of
the Adige, through the gate of Venice, the gate
through which the Veronese expected to see the
victorious Austrian army enter. From that moment
no one expected any serious defeat of the French.
" It would not be easy," Napoleon himself said, " to
conceive the surprise and enthusiasm of the inhabitants. Even the most hostile could not remain cold ;
and they added their congratulations to those of our
friends." The stupefaction of some, the delight of
others, were blended in the common transport, as if
a miracle had happened.

# VIII.

BONAPARTE had done wonders, and was himself amazed at his good fortune. He felt that henceforth he was in possession of that indefinable power which is mightier than any other, and is called prestige. Edgar Quinet says in his *Revolution:* "Napoleon has recorded that his high ambition came to him at Arcole, but he does not say why. I think I know the reason. Other victories, such as those of Montenotte, Lodi, Lonato, Castiglione, had been more complete. Why is it, then, that only at Arcole his star first appeared to him? It is because he had never been in such desperate straits. The invincible Army of Italy was about to lose the fruits of all its victories! And what would become of his fame, which eclipsed everything? It would be a mere ephemeral glory, with no substance, no future! To retreat would have been to lose, with Italy, much more than the result of so many prodigies; it would have meant his ruin. He would have flashed before the world for a moment, to sink into oblivion. Fortune would have smiled upon him merely in order to destroy him. Such might have been his thoughts, November 14, 1796. That day everything seemed lost, — prestige, confidence, glory, the Consulate, the Empire. The next day all had changed. It was at this moment that Napoleon must have thought himself the creature of destiny; he must have felt, after recrossing the Adige at Ronco, that nothing was impossible for a man who thus changed and ruled by a glance the course of events; that he was the man who was needed, — the master of fate. Henceforth, where could his ambition halt? Where could he set a limit to his plans? The feeling of the fatality of his power was born and grew up at the same moment as that of his ruin, and universal dominion appeared before him in the reeds of Arcole."

Bonaparte had triumphed, and yet he was sad. His face was gloomy, and his talk betrayed his melancholy thoughts. In fact, men of great ambition are usually haunted by a sort of melancholy when once their ambition is gratified. The emptiness of human things is such that the draught which fills the cup of glory seems tasteless even to those who quaff it. The feeling of the shortness of life, of the uncertainty of hope, fills human conquerors with this gloomy spirit. The shadow of death floats over all their great feats. Besides, great efforts, gigantic struggles, are followed by hours of moral and physical exhaustion.

However brilliant the victory, military glory has its sad side, and the sight of the battle-field depresses the most eager. The cries of the wounded and dying, which the conquerors as well as the conquered hear in the silence of the night, arouse a melancholy echo. Napoleon, for all his stoicism and impassibility on the battle-field, had afterwards moments of tenderness.

He said at Saint Helena that once he was passing over a battle-field in Italy, on which the bodies of the dead were still lying. "In the moonlight and the unbroken quiet, suddenly there sprang out from under the cloak of a corpse, a dog which ran towards us and then returned at once, uttering doleful cries; he licked his master's face a few times and then sprang at us again. He was asking aid and seeking vengeance." The Emperor went on: "Was it my state of mind, the place, the hour, the act itself? whatever it was, I can truly say that never has anything on the battle-field made such an impression on me. I stopped involuntarily to gaze at this spectacle. 'This man,' I thought, 'has friends, in the camp, perhaps, in his company, and here he lies abandoned by all except his dog. What a lesson nature gives us by means of this animal!... What is man! How mysterious are his impressions!' I had without emotion given the orders which were to decide the fate of the army; I had watched dry-eyed the execution of the movements which were to cause death to a great many of us; and here I was moved and deeply touched by this dog's howling.... What is certain is that at that moment I would have been very gentle to a suppliant foe, and I understood clearly how Achilles restored Hector's body when Priam wept."

Never, perhaps, did Bonaparte's disposition to revery and melancholy show itself more clearly than after Arcole. He wrote to Carnot from Verona, November 19, 1796: "Never was a battle-field more hotly contested than that of Arcole. I have scarcely any generals left. Their devotion and courage are unprecedented. General Lannes entered the action while still suffering from his wound, and was wounded besides twice after the first day. At three in the afternoon he was lying down in great pain, when he heard that I was taking a position at the head of the column. He sprang from his bed, and joined me on the bridge of Arcole, when a new wound felled him to the ground unconscious. I assure you the victory required all that."

The same day Bonaparte wrote to Clarke: "Your nephew, Elliot, was killed on the battle-field of Arcole. This young man had learned to know war. He has often marched at the head of our columns. . . . He died gloriously in front of the enemy. He did not suffer a moment. What reasonable man would not desire such a death? Who, in our uncertain life, would not deem himself happy to leave in that way a world which is often contemptible? Who is there of us who has not a hundred times regretted that he could not thus escape the stings of calumny, of envy, and of all the odious passions which seem alone to rule men's conduct?"

Physical suffering added to the melancholy which was stamped on Bonaparte's pale face. He was still tormented by a skin disease which he had caught at the siege of Toulon, when he seized a rammer from the hands of an artillery-man who was afflicted with the itch, and himself loaded the cannon ten or twelve times. The poison disturbed his nervous organization and infected his whole system. At about the time of Arcole, he suffered from the first attacks of another ailment, which sixteen years later was to diminish his activity and give him real alarm. Yvan, who was his surgeon until 1814, told General de Ségur, that in 1796 and 1797 he could only put an end to Napoleon's attacks by plunging him, there being no bath-tub, into the first barrel of water that he could lay his hands on.

In spite of wonderful triumphs, the conqueror of Arcole was suffering in mind and body. At certain moments he doubted Josephine's love, and this doubt was anguish. November 24, 1796, he wrote from Verona to his beloved wife : " Soon, my dear one, I hope to be in your arms. I love you madly. I am writing to Paris by this courier. All is well. Wurmser was defeated yesterday under Mantua. Your husband needs only Josephine's love to make him perfectly happy." Then he left Verona, without sending her word, to spend forty-eight hours with her at Milan. To his surprise and disappointment, she was not there. Then he wrote to her, seeing himself deprived of this longed-for meeting which he had hoped would be the most welcome prize of victory: "I reached Milan, rushed to your rooms, having thrown up everything to see you, to press you to my heart — you were not there; you are travelling about from one town to another, amusing yourself with balls: you go away from me when I arrive; you care no more for your dear Napoleon. A caprice made you love me; inconstancy makes you indifferent. I am accustomed to danger, and know the cure for the fatigues and evils of life. My unhappiness is inconceivable; I had no reason to expect it. I shall be here until the 9th [Frimaire]. Don't put yourself out; pursue your pleasure; happiness is made for you. The whole world is too happy if it can please you, and your husband alone is very, very unhappy."

When Bonaparte was thus lamenting, Josephine was at Genoa, where she had thought it her duty to accept an invitation from the city. "She was received," says Sir Walter Scott, "with studied magnificence by those in that ancient state who adhered to the French interest, and where, to the scandal of the rigid Catholics, the company continued assembled, at a ball given by M. de Serva, till a late hour on Friday morning, despite the presence of a senator having in his pocket, but not venturing to enforce, a decree of the senate for the better observation of the fast day upon the occasion."

Another letter from Bonaparte to Josephine, November 28: "I have received the despatches forwarded by Berthier from Genoa. I see clearly that

you didn't have time to write to me. In all your
pleasures and amusements, you would have done
wrong to sacrifice anything for me. Berthier has
been kind enough to show me the letter you wrote to
him. I have no intention of interfering with your
plans, or with the pleasure-parties that are offered to
you; I am not worth the trouble, and the happiness
or misery of a man whom you do not love has no
right to interest you. For me, to love you alone, to
make you happy, to do nothing that can annoy you,
that is the lot and aim of my life. Be happy, make
me no reproaches, do not trouble yourself about the
happiness of a man who lives only in your life, and
knows no other pleasures and joys than yours. When
I ask of you a love like mine, I am wrong. Why expect lace to weigh as much as gold? When I sacrifice to you all my desires, all my thoughts, every
moment of my life, I yield to the power which your
charms, your character, and your whole person exercise over my unhappy heart. It is my misfortune
that nature has denied me qualities that might fascinate you; but what I deserve to receive from Josephine is respect and esteem, for I love her madly and
I love her alone."

This passionately eloquent letter concludes with
this outbreak of affection: "Good by, you adorable
woman; good by, Josephine! Fate may crowd every
sorrow and suffering upon my heart, if only it will
give happy and bright days to Josephine. Who deserves them better than she? When there is no

longer any doubt possible that she has ceased to love me, I shall hide my crushing grief, and be satisfied to be able to be of some use to her, of some service. I open my letter to send you a kiss. . . . Oh, Josephine, Josephine !"

A few days later they met at Milan, and Bonaparte's agitated heart tasted a few moments of comparative peace. Lavalette, who was his aide-de-camp at that time, describes him at headquarters in Milan after Arcole: " I presented myself before the commander-in-chief, who was living in the Serbelloni palace, on a day of reception. The drawing-room was full of officers of all degrees, and of the high officials of the country. His manner was pleasant, but his glance was so haughty and piercing that I felt myself turn pale when he spoke to me. I stammered out my name and a few words of gratitude which he listened to in silence, with his eyes fixed on me and a severe expression which thoroughly confused me. At last he said: ' Come back at six o'clock and get the scarf.' This scarf, which was the distinguishing mark of the commander-in-chief's aides, was of white and red silk, and was worn on the left arm."

At that time, Bonaparte had eight aides-de-camp. Murat, who had just been promoted to the post of general, was no longer one of them. The first was Colonel Junot, who was as remarkable for his bravery and energy as for his ready wit. " While constructing one of the first batteries at Toulon against the English," we read in the *Memorial of Saint Helena,*

"Napoleon called for a sergeant or corporal who knew how to write. A young soldier stepped out of the ranks and resting the paper on the breastwork wrote at his dictation. As soon as the letter was finished, a shot covered it with earth. 'Good!' said the writer; 'I sha'n't need any sand.' This jest and the calmness with which it was uttered attracted Napoleon's attention and made the sergeant's fortune. He was Junot, afterwards Duke of Abrantès, General of Hussars, Commander in Portugal, Governor-General of Illyria."

The second aide was Marmont, later the Duke of Ragusa, a colonel of artillery, a descendant of an old and respected family of Burgundy. Marmont, who had received an excellent education, was distinguished for an intense love of glory, an unbounded ambition, and enthusiastic devotion to his chief. Later, the Duke of Ragusa thus described in his Memoirs this part of his life: "We were all very young, from our commander down to the humblest of his officers; our ambition was noble and pure; no trace of envy, no base passion, ever entered our hearts; a genuine friendship held us together, and our mutual attachment amounted to devotion. Our perfect confidence in the future, and our certainty about our destinies, inspired that philosophical spirit which contributes materially to happiness, and our invariable harmony made us a most united family. Finally, the variety of our occupations and our pleasures, the constant demand upon our physical and

mental qualities, lent to our life an interest and fulness which were most extraordinary."

Less brilliant than Junot and Marmont, but of a
solid character, was the third aide-de-camp, Duroc,
later Grand Marshal to the Palace, and Napoleon's
most trusted friend. He was killed by a cannon-ball
at Wurtschen; his death left on Bonaparte's spirit
so deep an impression that, when he was about to
embark upon the *Bellerophon* in 1815, the Emperor
asked permission to live as a private citizen in England under the name of Colonel Duroc.

The fourth aide-de-camp was the young Lemerrois,
who was scarcely seventeen years old and already
covered with wounds. The fifth was Sulkowski,
a Pole, an adventurous, chivalrous, and romantic
character. He spoke every European language.
After having fought for the freedom of Poland, and
having been wounded at the siege of Warsaw, he
entered the French army, and was greeted by Napoleon's soldiers as a fellow-countryman. The sixth
aide-de-camp was the brother of the commander-in-
chief, Louis Bonaparte, scarcely seventeen years old,
who was entrusted with the most dangerous duties.
These he performed with a zeal and heartiness that
showed how well he supported the burden of a great
name. The future King of Holland had a gentle
nature, his manners were simple, his character was
serious, he was prone to revery, and remarkably cool
in the hour of danger. At the battle of Arcole his
courage and devotion had been of service in saving

his brother's life. "Louis loved glory," said Napoleon at Saint Helena; "perhaps he loved me more." The seventh aide-de-camp was Croissier, a brave and skilful cavalry officer who had just taken the place of the young Elliot, who had met a glorious death at Arcole. The eighth and last was Lavalette, later Postmaster-General, who was condemned to death and confined in the Conciergerie at the second restoration, and only saved from execution by the devotion of his wife, who, to secure his escape, visited him in prison and sent him out dressed in her clothes.

Bonaparte's staff was already a sort of military court, of exceptional charm on account of its young and martial air. "The commander-in-chief," Lavalette says elsewhere, "was then happy in his wife's society. Madame Bonaparte was charming, and all the cares of the chief command, all the duties of government, could not prevent her husband from giving himself up to domestic happiness. It was during this short sojourn at Milan that the young painter Gros made the first portrait that exists of the general. He represented him on the bridge of Lodi at the moment when, flag in hand, he flung himself before his men to urge them on. The artist could never get the general to sit. Madame Bonaparte took her husband on her lap, after breakfast, and held him for a few minutes. I was present at these sittings; the age of the happy couple, the artist's modesty and his enthusiasm for the hero, excused this familiarity." Gros, thus painting Bonaparte's portrait at Milan, after the battle of Arcole, might make a good subject of a picture of one of our modern artists.

# IX.

## THE END OF THE CAMPAIGN.

THE Count of Las Cases recounts in the *Memorial* this conversation which he had with Napoleon at Saint Helena: "We said to the Emperor, speaking of the Italian campaign and the swift and daily victories which had made it so famous, that he must have got great pleasure out of it. 'None at all,' he replied. 'But at least Your Majesty gave some to those who were at a distance.' 'Possibly; at a distance one reads about the triumphs and ignores the state of things. If I had had any pleasure, I should have rested; but I always had danger in front of me, and the day's victory was at once forgotten in the necessity of winning a new one the next day.'"

Early in 1797 the war had to be resumed, and Bonaparte, who had caught a fever by bivouacking in a marsh near Mantua, was in a state of illness and exhaustion which filled the army with despair. Stendhal describes his appearance at the time, with his hollow, livid cheeks, which inspired the émigrés to say, "He is of a most beautiful yellow!" and they drank to his speedy death. "Only his eyes and their piercing glance announced the great man. This glance had won for him the confidence of the army, which forgave him for his feeble appearance, loving him only the better for it. They often compared their little corporal with the superb Murat, and their preference was for the puny general who had already won so great glory."

Austria was about to make a final effort. The great cities of that empire were sending battalions of volunteers. Those of Vienna had received from the Empress banners embroidered by her own hands.

Bonaparte was at Bologna, January 10, 1797, when he heard that the Austrians, to the number of sixty thousand men, were advancing by Montebaldo and the Paduan plains. In the night between the 13th and 14th of January he was on the eminence of Rivoli. The weather had cleared after very heavy rain. In the moonlight the general examined the lines of the enemy's camp-fires, which filled the whole region between the Adige and Lake Garda: the air was all ablaze with them. The bivouac fires indicated forty or fifty thousand Austrians. The next morning at six, there were to be at Rivoli only twenty-two thousand French troops. Never did Bonaparte show more amazing rapidity of conception, decision, and execution. January 14, he won the battle of Rivoli; he marched all that night with Masséna's division, which had won the victory; the evening of the 15th, he was before Mantua; the 16th, he won the battle of Favorita. In three days the

Austrian army, reduced to half its original size, completely disorganized, weakened by a multitude of killed and wounded, had lost twenty-two thousand men taken prisoners, its artillery, and baggage. Masséna's division had marched and fought incessantly for four days, marching by night and fighting by day. Bonaparte could boast that his soldiers had surpassed the famous speed of Cæsar's legions. "The Roman legions," he wrote at the time, "used to make twenty-four miles a day; our men make thirty and fight in the intervals." He also wrote to Carnot: "The esteem of a few such men as you, that of my comrades and the soldiers, sometimes, too, the opinion of posterity, and above all, the state of my own conscience, and the prosperity of my country, alone interest me." February 3, Wurmser surrendered at Mantua. Bonaparte, who had accorded honorable conditions to the venerable Austrian general, was unwilling to be present at the scene of his humiliation, and was already in the Romagna when he and his staff marched out before the French troops. The studied indifference with which Bonaparte denied himself the agreeable spectacle of a marshal of a great reputation, the commander-in-chief of the Austrian forces, at the head of his staff, giving up his sword, was a matter of surprise to all Europe. A few days later he wrote to the Directory: "I was anxious to show French generosity to Wurmser, a general more than seventy years old, to whom fortune has been unkind, but who has never ceased to show a constancy and a courage that history will not forget."

The war with Austria came to a pause; that with the Holy See continued. February 10, Bonaparte wrote to Josephine as follows: " We have been at Ancona for two days. We captured the citadel by a sudden attack, after a little firing. We took twelve hundred prisoners. I have sent fifty officers to their homes. I am still at Ancona. I don't send for you, because our work is not done yet; but I hope it will be finished in a few days. Besides, the country is very hostile, and everybody is afraid. I leave for the mountains to-morrow. You never write; and yet you ought to send me a line every day. I beg of you to take a walk every day; it will do you good. I have never been so tired of anything as I am with this horrid war. Good by, my dear. Think of me." February 13, he wrote again from Ancona: " I hear nothing from you, and I am sure that you don't love me. I have sent you newspapers and different letters. I am leaving at once, to cross the mountains. The moment anything is settled, I shall send for you: that is my most earnest desire. Thousands and thousands of kisses." February 16, three days before the signing of the Treaty of Tolentino, he wrote from Bologna: " You are gloomy; you are ill; you don't write to me; you want to go to Paris. Don't you love your husband any more? This thought makes me very unhappy. My dear one, I find life unendurable, since I hear of your low spirits. I hasten to send Mascati, that he may pre-scribe for you. My health is not very good: my cold holds on. I beg of you to take care of yourself, to love me as much as I love you, and to write to me every day. You can't imagine how uneasy I am. I have told Mascati to escort you to Ancona, if you desire to go there. I will send you word where I am. Perhaps I shall make peace with the Pope, and be with you soon: that is my most ardent wish. I send you a hundred kisses. Remember that nothing equals my love, except my uneasiness. Write to me every day. Good by, my dear."

February 19, Bonaparte signed the Treaty of To-lentino with the Pope. He was but three days' march from the capital; and nothing would have been easier for him than to enter the Eternal City in triumph. He was wise enough to decide otherwise.

At this period he thought it best to be gentle towards religion. Prince Metternich has observed in his Memoirs : "Napoleon was not irreligious in the ordinary sense of the word. He did not acknowl-edge that there had ever existed a sincere atheist; he condemned deism as the result of rash specula-tion. As a Christian and a Catholic, he assigned only to an established religion the right of governing human society. He regarded Christianity as the corner-stone of all true civilization, and Catholicism as the religion most favorable to the preservation of the order and peace of the moral world; Protestant-ism he looked upon as a source of trouble and discord.

He compelled the Pope to cede Avignon and the Venaissin, Bologna, Ferrara, and the Romagna, and to pay a subsidy of thirty millions. But at the same time, he wrote to him this respectful letter, quite unlike the usual language of France during the Revolution: "I must thank Your Holiness for the courteous expressions contained in the letter which you have been kind enough to write to me. Peace has just been signed between the French Republic and Your Holiness. I am glad to have been able to contribute to his personal repose. All Europe is aware of the pacific and conciliatory disposition of Your Holiness! The French Republic will be, I hope, one of the truest friends of Rome. I send my aide-de-camp to convey to Your Holiness the unfailing esteem and veneration which I feel for his person."

The same day the peace of Tolentino was concluded, February 19, 1797, Bonaparte wrote the following letter to Josephine, who was then at Bologna: "Peace has just been signed with Rome. Bologna, Ferrara, the Romagna, are ceded to the Republic. The Pope gives us shortly thirty millions and many works of art. I leave to-morrow morning for Ancona, and thence for Rimini, Ravenna, and Bologna. If your health permits, come to Rimini or Ravenna, but I beg of you, take care of yourself.

"Not a word from you; Heavens! what have I done? To think only of you, to love only Josephine, to know no other happiness than hers, does all that make me worthy of such a cruel fate? My dear, I beg of you, think of me often, and write every day. You must be ill, or you don't love me! Do you think my heart is made of marble? Do my sufferings move you so little? How little you know me! I should not have believed it. You to whom nature has given intelligence, gentleness, and beauty, you who rule alone over my heart, you who, doubtless, know only too well the absolute power you exercise over my heart, write to me, think of me, and love me. Ever yours."

This letter, dated February 19, at Tolentino, is printed in the collection published by Queen Hortense as the last written by Napoleon to Josephine during the first Italian campaign. It is much to be regretted that Josephine's letters to her husband have not also been preserved; but it is fair to suppose from Napoleon's repeated reproaches, that his wife wrote very cool answers to the sentimental effusions of her passionate husband. She was proud of him; she admired his glory, and was dazzled and fascinated by his success. Still we may doubt whether she loved him; and love, even between married people, cannot be commanded. If later Napoleon became less ardent, it may be because he was disappointed in the return which his love met. We should be inclined to think that Madame de Rémusat was not wholly mistaken when she thus expressed herself on this delicate subject: "Bonaparte's letters betray the emotions of a jealousy which varies between despondency and threats of violence. Then we find gloomy thoughts, a sort of disgust with the passing illusions of life. Possibly the cold reception with which his ardent feelings were met had its influence upon and at last benumbed him. Perhaps he would have been a better man if he had been more, and especially better, loved." Moreover, it may well be that Josephine's coldness was the result of calculation. There are men who are more fascinated by indifference than by surrender, and who prefer a changing sky to the monotonous blue of doting love. We must not forget that Josephine had to deal with a conqueror, and that love is like war. She never yielded; she let herself be won; had she been more tender, more loving, possibly Bonaparte might have loved her less.

The war was not yet over. Austria, with its inexhaustible resources, was perpetually renewing the struggle. Its armies were ever springing from the ground. After Beaulieu, Wurmser; after Wurmser, Alvinzy; after Alvinzy, the Archduke Charles. This German prince, who had won his spurs in Germany, came to Italy. Bonaparte, with thirty thousand men, hastened to encounter him, in a bitter cold, over mountains covered with snow. March 13, 1797, he crossed the Piave; the 16th, he defeated the Archduke in the battle of Tagliamento; soon he arrived at Gradisca; a few days later he took Laybach and Trieste; the 26th, he entered Germany; the 29th, he captured Klagenfurt. Whether from fatigue and physical exhaustion or from prudence and craft, he felt that the hour of peace had struck. He had won enough fame as a soldier; now he was to appear as a peacemaker.

This unrivalled manager understood how to arrange peace with as much art as he had shown in carrying on war. After crossed swords, the olive-branch; after fury, moderation; after glory, peace and rest. France was all aflame for this young man who flattered in turn its glory and its interest, and kept such close touch with public opinion. March 31, he wrote to the Archduke Charles a letter, replete with philosophy and the love of humanity after the fashion of the time, and its publication, a few days later in the *Moniteur* had an enormous effect. In it Bonaparte said: " General, brave soldiers make war, but love peace. . . . Have we killed enough men and done enough harm to humanity? This sixth campaign begins under unhappy auspices; whatever may be its issue, we shall kill between us, a few thousand men more, and we must at last come to an understanding, since everything, even human passions, has an end. . . . You, General, who by birth are so near the throne, and so superior to the petty passions which often animate ministers and governments, are you determined to deserve the title of the Saviour of Germany ? . . . As for me, if the overture which I have the honor of making to you, can save one man's life, I shall be prouder of the civic crown which I shall deem myself to have earned, than of all the sad glory which may come from military triumphs."

April 15, Bonaparte arrived at Leoben. His advance seized the Semmering; the French were only twenty-five leagues from Vienna. The Archduke Charles requested a suspension of hostilities. Bonaparte acceded, and, April 18, he signed the preliminaries of a peace on the following conditions: Belgium and the left bank of the Rhine to be ceded to France; cession of Lombardy for the purpose of making it an independent state, in consideration of an indemnity to Austria from the Venetian territory. Towards the end of April he returned to Italy, and when he reached Treviso, May 3, an order of the day was published, in which he declared war against the Venetian Republic, which had declared against him before the preliminaries of Leoben, and had seen French soldiers massacred. General Baragney d'Hilliers seized the lagoons, forts, and batteries of Venice, and, May 16, hoisted the tricolor flag in the Piazza of Saint Mark. Bonaparte had returned to Milan.

# X.

## THE SERBELLONI PALACE.

THE spring of 1797 was perhaps the happiest time in the lives of Napoleon and Josephine. The poet Arnault, when he came from Paris in May, found the two at Milan, settled in the Serbelloni Palace, which at that time attracted more attention from all Europe than did the residences of emperors and kings. The Duke of Serbelloni, a convert to the French notions of liberty, was proud to have under his roof the hero of Arcole, who was then looked on as the restorer of Italian liberty. The Duke's palace, with its blocks of finished granite all sparkling with small crystals, its vast and sumptuous drawing-rooms, its lofty colonnades, its wide, long gallery, was one of the most luxurious residences of Milan. Arnault sets before us Bonaparte with his military court in a drawing-room where were Josephine and a few pretty women: Madame Visconti, Madame Leopold Berthier, Madame Yvan. Near the ladies was Eugene de Beau-harnais, on a sofa, jesting as merrily as a page. The general made his appearance, and every one stood up. Berthier, Kilmaine, Clarke, and Augereau waited for a glance, a word, the slightest sign. The group gathered about Bonaparte, and he began to tell stories, to explain his victories, talking at one moment on military matters, and the next, philosophy and poetry. "To the interest of these remarks," Arnault goes on in his Souvenirs, "uttered now with a serious voice, and now with animation, must be added the authority that is given by a singularly mobile face, the severe expression of which is often tempered by the kindliest smile, by a look which reflects the deepest thoughts of a most powerful intelligence and the warmest feelings of a most passionate heart, — to all this must be added the charm of a melodious and manly voice, and then it will be possible to conceive how easily Bonaparte won by his conversation those whom he desired to fascinate." He had just been talking for two hours steadily, standing all the time, like the listeners, and no one had felt a moment's fatigue. As he left, Arnault said to Regnauld de Saint Jean d'Angely: "That man is an exceptional being; everything succumbs to his superior genius, to the force of his character; everything about him bears the stamp of authority. You notice how his authority is recognized by the people, who submit to him without knowing it, or perhaps in spite of themselves. What an expression of respect and admiration the men wear who approach him! He is born to command, as so many others to obey. If he is not lucky enough to be carried off by a bullet before four years from now, he will be in exile or on the throne."

Josephine was already like a queen. She will confess later that nothing ever equalled the impression which she received at this time, when, according to Madame de Rémusat, "love seemed to come every day to place at her feet a new conquest over a people entranced with its conqueror." Bonaparte was then the favorite of the populace of Milan. They used to wait for hours to see him come out of the Serbelloni Palace. The Italians, who, like the rest of the world, are devoted to success, applauded the young general all the more enthusiastically because they regarded him as one of themselves. "Everything," he said one day, "even my foreign origin, which was brought up against me in France, has been of service to me. It caused me to be regarded as a fellow-countryman by the Italians, and greatly aided my success in Italy. When I had obtained my success, people began to look up the history of a family which had long fallen into obscurity. It was found, as all Italians knew, to have long played an important part with them. In their estimation it had become an Italian family, so much so that when the question came up of my sister Pauline's marriage with Prince Borghese, there was only one opinion in Rome and in Tuscany, in that family and all its branches. 'It's all right,' they said; 'it's between ourselves; it's one of our families.' Later, when the question arose of the Pope's crowning me in Paris, this important matter encountered serious difficulties: the Austrian party in the Conclave opposed it violently; the Italian

party prevailed by adding to the political consideration the force of national pride : ' After all,' they said,
' it's an Italian family that we are establishing over
the barbarians ; we shall be avenged for the Goths.' "

At Milan, as in Paris, Josephine was of great service to her husband's plans. She helped him play his
double part now as a revolutionary leader, now as a
conservative. When he wished to oppose royalism,
he made use of men with the ideas of Augereau; when
he wanted to cajole people of the old régime, Josephine, by her antecedents, her relations, her character,
was the bond of union between him and the European
aristocracy. He acknowledged this himself.

" My marriage with Madame de Beauharnais,"
said Napoleon, " brought me into relations with a
party which I required for my plan of fusion, which
was one of the most important principles of my
administration, and one of the most characteristic.
Had it not been for my wife, I should not have had
any easy means of approaching it."

The drawing-room of the former Viscountess of
Beauharnais, in the Serbelloni Palace, recalled the
elegance and the traditions of the most brilliant
drawing-rooms of the Faubourg Saint Germain. Josephine used to receive there the Milanese nobility
with exquisite grace, and exercised a formal etiquette
in marked contrast with the very demagogic tone of
the addresses issued by the Army of Italy before the
18th Fructidor. Thanks to his Italian shrewdness,
Bonaparte knew how to please both the *sansculottes*

and those who wore knee-breeches. He intrigued as skilfully with the most ardent democrats as with the ambassadors of the old courts of Austria and Naples.

At one time he would be taken for a mounted tribune; at another, for a potentate. According to some, he was a Brutus; according to others, he was soon to be a Cæsar. There is nothing more interesting than to study him in this double aspect. While Bonaparte's lieutenants used the most revolutionary language, he himself, in confidential talk with his intimates, expressed contempt for the methods of the demagogue. This commander-in-chief, who had been appointed by the Directory, already felt for the Directors, and especially for Barras, his especial patron, the most profound scorn; but if such were his thoughts, he took care to hide them. The time had not come for throwing off his mask. Josephine, who was very intimate with Barras, helped, possibly without knowing it, to allay the discord which otherwise could not have failed to arise between the Director and the young, indocile general. Barras, by expressing any discontent with Bonaparte, who often disobeyed the instructions of the Directory, would have feared to wound his friend Josephine, who was so charming at the festivities of the Luxembourg. Thus it was that she continued at Milan the work she had begun in Paris; and in fact, she was Bonaparte's mainstay with the Directory.

Josephine was at that time thirty-four years old. Her somewhat brown and faded complexion was dis-

guised by rouge and powder, which she employed
with great skill; the smallness of her mouth concealed the badness of her teeth: she remedied her
natural defects by art. The elegance of her figure,
her graceful movements, her refined expression, her
soft eyes and gentle voice, her dignified bearing,
and all the harmony of her person, gave her an exceptional charm. Moreover, an air of coquetry, which
was all the more attractive because it seemed natural
and involuntary; an indolence, which was but another
fascination; her unpretending but always pleasing
conversation; her unfailing kindness; manners that
recalled the best traditions of the court of Versailles;
great taste in dress; toilettes and jewels that queens
might have envied, — all these things enable us to
understand the power which so attractive a woman
was able to exercise over Bonaparte's intelligence
and heart. He was absolutely faithful to her; and
this at a time when there was not a beauty in Milan
who was not setting her cap for him. His loyalty to
her was partly a matter of love, partly of calculation.
As he himself said, "his position was most delicate;
he commanded old generals; jealous eyes spied his
every movement; he was extremely circumspect.
His fate depended on his conduct; he might have
forgotten himself for an hour, and how many of his
victories hung on no more than that brief space of
time!"

Many years later, at the time of his coronation at
Milan, the celebrated singer, Grassini, attracted his

attention; circumstances were less austere; he sent for her, and after the first moment of a speedy acquaintance, she reminded him that she had made her first appearance at exactly the time of his first exploits as commander of the Army of Italy. "I was then in the full flower of my beauty and talent. No one talked of anything except of me in the *Virgins of the Sun.* I charmed every one. The young general alone was indifferent, and he alone interested me. How strange! When I really was somebody, and all Italy at my feet, I scorned it all for one of your glances. I could not win it, and now you let them fall on me when I am no longer worthy of you or them."

In May, 1797, Bonaparte was relatively happy, — as happy as could be a man of his ardent and restless nature, for whom peace and happiness seemed not to exist. A few days had been enough to restore his strength after all his emotions, fatigues, and perils. The suspicions he had felt about his wife were speedily dissipated; and Josephine at last became accustomed to Italy, where she held so lofty a position, and her pride was thoroughly gratified.

As for the French army, it was wild with joy over its triumphs. Milan seemed its Paradise. Stendhal has written a most picturesque description of this enchanting period, when the officers and soldiers were all young and loving, the ladies of Milan were each more beautiful and more amiable than another. There was the promenade of the Corso on the bastion

of the eastern gate, that old Spanish rampart planted
with chestnut-trees and forty feet above the green
plain; and there fashionable society used to meet
every day — the women in low carriages called
*bastardelles.*

Before the French army reached Milan, there had
never been more than two lines of carriages in the
Corso; afterwards there were always four, sometimes
six, filling the whole length of the promenade. At
the centre the carriages as they arrived took their
single turn, at a gentle trot. Happy were the staff or
cavalry officers who could dash into this labyrinth:
they were objects of envy to the infantry officers.
But when, as the evening comes on, and the hour of
the *Ave Maria*, the carriages start again, and the
ladies, without alighting, eat ices in front of a
fashionable café, then the infantry officers have
their innings at the entrance of the café of the
*Corsia de' Servi.* Some have come ten leagues to
be at the rendezvous. Fridays, when the theatres
used to be closed, there was a ball at the casino of
the Albergo della Città: every other evening there
were magnificent performances at the Scala. The
ladies of Milan received in their boxes a number of
French officers, thereby driving their *cavalieri ser-
venti* to despair as they saw the attentions showered
on the young conquerors. The pit was also filled
with officers who were not happy enough to be
invited into the boxes; but they were not discouraged
by that, and they cast tender and respectful glances

on the objects of their adoration.  Men who knew no shadow of fear in the face of shells and bullets blushed and trembled before a woman.  They scarcely dared to raise their eyes to the boxes where shone, like stars, the ladies whom they worshipped.  If their suit was hopeless, these ladies would look at them through the large end of their opera-glasses, which put them off at a distance; if, however, they looked at them through the other end, which brought them nearer, then they were filled with happiness!

> " *O primavera, gioventù dell' anno !*
>   *O gioventù, primavera della vita !* '

> "O spring, youth of the year !
>   O youth, springtime of life ! "

# XI.

## THE COURT OF MONTEBELLO.

WHEN the hot weather set in, Bonaparte and his wife took up their quarters at the castle of Montebello, a few leagues from Milan, at the top of a hill from which there was a wide view over the rich plains of Lombardy. There they remained three months, holding a sort of diplomatic and military court, which the Italians, discerning the future sovereign under the Republican general, called the court of Montebello. In fact, Bonaparte had already assumed the airs of a monarch. Every one wondered that he had in so brief a time acquired such glory and could exercise so great influence in Europe. Scarcely thirteen months before, as an unknown general he had taken command at Nice of an army destitute of everything, and now holding the position of conqueror in the most beautiful region of the world, surrounded by the ministers of Austria and Naples, the envoys of the Pope, of the King of Sardinia, of the Republics of Genoa and Venice, he had become the arbiter of the destinies of Italy. Let us hear what an eyewitness, the Count Miot de Mélito, says: "It was in the magnificent castle of Montebello that I found Bonaparte, rather in the midst of a brilliant court than at the headquarters of an army. Already there prevailed a rigid etiquette; his aides-de-camp and officers were no longer received at his table, and he was very particular about what guests he received there: this was a much-sought-for honor, and one only obtained with great difficulty. He dined, so to speak, in public; during his meals there were admitted into the dining-room the inhabitants of the country, who gazed at him with the greatest interest However, he betrayed no embarrassment or confusior. at this extreme honor, and received them as if he had been accustomed to it all his life. His drawing-rooms and a large tent that he had had built in front of the castle, on the side of the gardens, were constantly filled with a crowd of generals, officials, and purvey ors, as well as with the highest nobles and the most distinguished men of Italy, who came to solicit the favor of a glance or a moment's interview."

Austria had sent as its plenipotentiaries to the court of Montebello two great nobles: an Austrian, the Count of Mersfeld; and a Neapolitan, the Marquis of Gallo, ambassador from Naples at Vienna, the same who later was ambassador at Paris, and Minister of Foreign Affairs in the reign of Joseph Bonaparte, King of Naples, as well as of Murat, who succeeded him on the throne.

At this time Bonaparte had with him his brothers, Joseph and Louis, his sister Pauline, and his mother,

Madame Letitia, who had just come from Marseilles and Genoa with two of her daughters: Elisa, later Duchess of Tuscany, and Caroline, afterwards Queen of Naples. As they passed through Genoa, they found that city in tremendous excitement.

It was the very moment when Lavalette, one of Bonaparte's aides-de-camp, had handed to the Doge, before the full Senate, this letter, dated May 27, 1797: "If, within twenty-four hours after the reception of this letter, which I send to you by one of my aides-de-camp, you shall not have placed all the Frenchmen who are in your prison at the disposition of the French Ministry; if you shall not have had arrested the men who are exciting the people of Genoa against the French; if, finally, you do not disarm this populace, which will be the first to rise against you when it shall have perceived the terrible consequences of the errors into which you will have led it, — the Minister of the French Republic will leave Genoa, and the aristocracy will have existed. The heads of the Senators will guarantee to me the security of all the Frenchmen who are in Genoa, and the united states of the Republic will guarantee their property. I beg of you, in conclusion, to have perfect confidence in the feelings of esteem and distinguished consideration which I nourish for Your Highness's person."

Never before that day had a stranger entered the Senate Chamber. The excitement of the city rendered wild excesses probable. Since Bonaparte had

not received the letter announcing the arrival in
Italy of his mother and sisters, no precautions had
been taken, no orders had been given.   Madame Letitia might easily be the victim of an uprising of the
populace.   Lavalette's first thought was to stay with
them, and to defend as well as he could, in case of
attack; but Madame Bonaparte was a woman of
great sense and courage.   "I have nothing to fear
here, so long as my son holds the leading citizens of
the Republic as hostages.   Go back, and tell him
of my arrival: to-morrow morning I shall continue
my journey."   Lavalette followed her advice, simply
taking the precaution of letting a few cavalry pickets
ride ahead of the three ladies.   They reached Milan
without accident, and the next day took up their
quarters at the castle of Montebello.

Madame Letitia, who was a very proud woman,
was highly pleased to see her son enjoying so much
power and glory.   As Sir Walter Scott says in his
*Life of Napoleon Bonaparte*, "every town, every village, desired to distinguish itself by some peculiar mark
of homage and respect to him, whom they named the
Liberator of Italy. . . .   Honor beyond that of a
crowned head was his own, and had the full relish
of novelty to a mind which two or three years before
was pining in obscurity.   Power was his, and he had
not experienced its cares and risks ; high hopes were
formed of him by all around, and he had not yet
disappointed them.   He was in the flower of youth,
and married to the woman of his heart.   Above all,

he had the glow of Hope, which was marshalling him
even to more exalted dominion; and he had not yet
become aware that possession brings satiety, and that
all earthly desires and wishes terminate, when fully
attained, in vanity and vexation of spirit."

The castle of Montebello was then a most agreeable and picturesque place. The excellence of the
climate, the beauty of the springtime, the entertainments, the banquets, the picnics, the excursions on
Lake Maggiore and Lake Como, — this perpetual
round of duties and pleasures, which give to life
variety and fulness, made the castle of Montebello
as fascinating as it was interesting. Arnault, in
his Souvenirs, describes a dinner there. During
the meal, the band of the Guides, the best band in
the army, played military marches and patriotic airs.
At table the poet sat next to Pauline Bonaparte,
then a girl of sixteen, who was soon to become
Madame Leclerc. "If," he says, "she was the pretti-
est person in the world, she was also the most frivolous. She had the manners of a schoolgirl, chattering
continually, giggling at everything and nothing,
imitating the most serious people, making faces at
her sister-in-law when she was not looking, poking
me with her knee when I did not pay enough attention to her gambols, and every now and then bringing
down on herself one of those terrible glances with
which her brother used to crush the most obdurate
men; the next minute she would begin again, and
the authority of the commander of the Army of

Italy succumbed before the giddiness of a young girl."

After dinner they drank coffee on the terrace, not going back to the drawing-room till late, and Bonaparte took part in the general conversation: he arranged the diversions of the company, making Madame Leopold Berthier sing, and asking General Clarke for stories; and he told some himself, preferring fantastic and terrifying incidents, terrible adventures, ghost stories, which he made more impressive by using his voice in a way that an actor might have envied. At the end of the evening many of the guests returned to Milan through the strangely illuminated country, for every field was ablaze with thousands of fire-flies which seemed to dance on the turf, springing four or five feet into the air.

"How many memories recur to me," says Marmont, later the Duke of Ragusa, "of this three months' stay at Montebello! What a busy, important, hopeful, and happy time it was! Then, ambition was a thing of minor importance; our duties and pleasures alone occupied us. We were all on the frankest and most cordial terms, and nothing occurred to mar our harmony." Surrounded by his family, his fellow-soldiers, his lieutenants, who were both his servants and his friends, Bonaparte, who then desired for every nation only peace, concord, and progress, was enjoying a moment of calm. Marmont describes him at this period, with the air of a master in his attitude, his expression, and his voice, and in public neglecting no opportunity to maintain and augment the universal feeling of respect and subjection; yet, in private life, with his mother, his wife, his brothers and sisters, his aides-de-camp, appearing kindly, affable even to the point of familiarity, fond of fun, yet never offensive, taking part in the sports of his fellow-officers, and even persuading the solemn Austrian plenipotentiaries to join in them; uttering with uncommon eloquence a number of new and interesting ideas, — in a word, " possessing at that happy time a charm to which no one could be insensible."

As for Josephine, whose grace and amiability attracted every one, she was trying, so to speak, to play naturally her next part as sovereign. The highest, the most beautiful, the most intelligent ladies of Milan, gathered about her, and admired the exquisite urbanity, the rare tact, and the unfailing kindness with which she did the honors of her drawing-room. "When she was leaving Martinique, an old fortune-teller had told her, 'You will be more than a queen.' Was this prophecy to be realized at once? She was adored by a man who aroused universal admiration, surrounded by everything that could delight a woman, and her brow had not yet felt the uneasiness the crown sometimes produces." [1]

Bonaparte continued to be fascinated by his wife, and this anecdote which Arnault tells will show

---

[1] *Memoirs concerning General Auguste de Colbert*, by his son, the Marquis Colbert de Chabanais.

Josephine's power over her husband. She had a little pug dog called Fortuné, of which she was extremely fond, though he reminded her of a time of great sorrow. When she was imprisoned, in the Reign of Terror, she was separated from the Viscount of Beauharnais, who was incarcerated elsewhere. Her children had permission to come to see her at the office, with their governess, but the jailer was always present at these meetings. It occurred to the governess to take Fortuné with her; and he made his way to Josephine's cell, carrying concealed in his collar a letter with all the news. After the 9th of Thermidor Josephine would never be parted from her pet. One day at Montebello he was lying on the sofa with his mistress. "You see that fellow there," said Bonaparte to Arnault, pointing at the dog; "he is my rival. When I married I wanted to put him out of my wife's room, but I was given to understand that I might go away myself or share it with him. I was annoyed, but it was to take or to leave, and I yielded. The favorite was not so accommodating, and he left his mark on this leg." Insolent like all favorites, Fortuné had great faults; he was continually barking and used to bite everybody, even other dogs. At Montebello he had the imprudence to bite the cook's dog, a surly mastiff, who with one turn of the head killed the little fellow. Josephine was in despair, and the unhappy cook thought himself ruined. A few days afterwards he met the general walking in the garden, and fled in terror. "Why do you run away from me in this way?" asked Bonaparte. "General, after what my dog did —" "Well?" "I was afraid that you would hate the sight of me." "Your dog! Haven't you him any longer?" "Excuse me, General, he never sets a paw in the garden, especially since Madame has another—" "Let him come in as much as he wants; perhaps he will make way with him too." The gentlest and most indolent of creoles intimidated the most wilful and despotic of men. Bonaparte might win battles, do miracles, create or destroy states, but he could not put a dog out of the room.

# XII.

ONE thing disturbed Bonaparte in the midst of all his success, and that was the perpetual attacks of the reactionary newspapers of Paris. The talk of the drawing-room, the sarcasms of the émigrés, the unceasing declamation of the Royalist Club in the rue de Clichy had the power of exasperating his irascible nature. Besides, he dreaded the Restoration, which was not to take place till seventeen years later, and more than one émigré spoke of it as imminent in 1797. Bonaparte was unwilling at any price to be the second. The part of a Monk had no temptation for him; and no title, no wealth, could have persuaded him to work for any one but himself. It is also to be borne in mind, that if he had assumed some aristocratic methods, and found pleasure in the society of people of the old régime, he commanded an army of the most ardent and most sincere Republicans. He had wrought such miracles with his men, only allying himself in appearance, if not in fact, with the political passions which were the mainspring of their energy and enthusiasm. In their eyes, their gen-

eral was always the man of the 13th Vendémiaire,
the terror of the reaction, the sturdy Republican
who had shattered the Royalist bands.  He thought
the time fitting for a grand Republican ceremony
which should impress every one by a spectacle in
harmony with the ideas and passions of the soldiers;
consequently he decided that July 14, 1797, the anni-
versary of the capture of the Bastille, he would ex-
hibit his troops at Milan under a purely Republican
aspect, and gave orders for a great military festival
upon that day, with a programme in perfect harmony
with the Revolutionary memories and democratic
sentiments of an army which contained so many
Jacobins.  This festival was to make an impression
in Paris and to serve as a prologue to the 18th
Fructidor.

This is a programme of the festival as it was
drawn up by the commander-in-chief: —

1.  At daybreak a salvo of twenty of the largest
cannon shall announce the festival.

2.  The general shall be beaten at nine in the morning.  At ten, when the troops start, another salvo
shall be fired.

3.  A third salvo shall announce the departure of
the commander-in-chief for the scene of the festival,
and another salvo shall be fired on his arrival.  At
the same time all the bands shall play the air, *Où
peut-on être mieux?*

4.  At noon precisely, the troops, after having made

some manœuvres, will form in a square about the Pyramid. Then first six cannon will be fired for each one of the generals, La Harpe, Stengel, and Dubois; then five for each brigadier-general; then for each adjutant-general and chief of brigade in the division killed since the 23d Germinal, Year IV., the date of the battle of Montenotte.

5. The general commanding the division of Lombardy will give the flags to each battalion, and six cannon shall be fired at the moment he presents them.

6. The men shall receive double pay, and double rations of meat and wine.

7. The festival will terminate with drill and exercise. First, artillery practice; then firing at a target. There will be three prizes given to the three best shots.

8. Then there will be a match with broadswords and with rapiers, followed by a foot-race with three prizes.

9. The regimental bands shall play tunes and dance-music, and the soldiers, having piled their arms, shall be free to stroll about until the drums recall them to the ranks.

10. Officers who own horses and care to enter them for the race must have their names registered. The course will be from the country-house from which the horses started at the last race, to the Arch of Triumph.

11. At nightfall the Pyramid and the Altar of Country shall be illuminated, and bands placed about shall play patriotic dances.

It was not among his soldiers alone, it was also among the Italians, that Bonaparte developed a love of arms and of physical exercise. The whole population of Milan was transformed. In the schools, the streets, the drawing-rooms, in children's games, education, habits, and public opinion, there was a complete change. At the theatre the Italian was no longer represented as beaten by the German matador; it was the Italian who beat and drove away the German. A martial air and a military spirit fascinated the women. Warlike marches took the place of religious songs and amorous serenades. Consequently, this celebration of July 14 enraptured the Milanese.

Bonaparte was never happier or prouder than when among his soldiers. Every regiment recalled happy memories. He had said at Lonato: "I was at ease; the 32d was there!" And for their sole reward the men of the 32d asked to have those few words embroidered on their regimental flag. In his account of the battle of Favorita, he had spoken of the " terrible 57th," and the proud 57th, fully rewarded for its losses by this one word, adopted henceforth the name of " The Terrible."

This celebration inflamed the pride and anger of the army; it was a great manifestation against Royalism. On the sides of a high pyramid were inscribed the names of the officers and men who had fallen on the field of honor since the battle of Montenotte. This funereal pyramid rose in the middle of a Field of Mars, which was decorated with all the attributes

representing the victories of the army, as well as the
emblems of liberty, of the French Republic one and
indivisible, and of the Constitution of the Year III.
After different manœuvres, the troops formed in a
square around the pyramid. The veterans and the
wounded marched by, saluted by the troops. Drums
were beating ; the roar of cannon was incessant. Then
the general reviewed the troops. When he had
reached the carabineers of the 11th Regiment of light
infantry, he said, " Brave carabineers, I am glad to
see you ; you alone are worth three thousand men."
In front of the 13th, which formed the garrison at
Verona, he exclaimed, " Brave soldiers, you see before you the names of your comrades murdered before
your eyes at Verona ; but their shades must be satisfied, — the tyrants have perished with their tyranny."
The officers of each regiment, preceded by the band,
went forward to receive the flags. " Citizens," said
the commander-in-chief, "may these banners always
be in the path of liberty and victory ! " While the
army was marching by, a corporal of the 9th Regiment
went up to Bonaparte, and said : " General, you have
saved France. Your men, proud to belong to an
invincible army, will make a rampart of their bodies.
Save the Republic ! Let the hundred thousand men
who compose this army crowd together in defence of
liberty." And tears ran down the brave soldier's face.

It is easy to imagine the enthusiasm of these heroes,
covered with wounds and laurel, proud, and justly
proud, of themselves, their courage, their triumphs,

and indignant with the sarcasms which certain Frenchmen did not blush to utter against all this glory and all these sacrifices, so much unselfishness, and so many wonders. Inspired by the fumes of powder, their general's Republican proclamation, and carried away by warlike ardor, the wild applause of the crowd, and the grand military spectacle before their eyes, by the clash of arms, the sight of the flags, the roar of artillery, the trumpets, the drums, and the patriotic hymns, on this warm 14th of July, Bonaparte's soldiers were wild with wrath against the blasphemous defamers of liberty and glory.

In the evening Bonaparte gave a dinner to the officers and veterans, at which he proposed this toast: " To the shades of the brave Stengel, who fell on the field of Mondovi ; of La Harpe, who died on the field of Formbio ; of Dubois, who died at Roveredo ; and to all the brave men who died in defence of liberty ! May their spirits ever be near us ! They will warn us of the ambushes set by the enemies of our country." This was General Berthier's toast: " To the Constitution of the Year III., and to the executive Directory of the French Republic ! May it, by its firmness, be worthy of the armies and high destinies of the Republic, and may it crush all the foes of the Revolution, who no longer mask themselves ! " The band played *Ça ira.* This was the toast of a veteran, all scarred with wounds, who had lost a limb: " To the re-emigration of the émigrés ! " Toast of General Lannes, still bearing the marks of three wounds he had received at Arcole : "To the destruction of the Club of Clichy! The wretches! They wish more revolutions. May the blood of the patriots they have assassinated fall on their own heads!" The band played a charge.

In the course of the day the different divisions of the Army of Italy had signed addresses which were sent to the Directory by Bonaparte, and inserted in the *Moniteur* of August 12.

This is the address of Masséna's division : "Does the road to Paris present more difficulties than that to Vienna? No. It will be opened by Republicans who have remained faithful to liberty ; we shall defend it, and enemies will have perished."

Division Augereau : "Is it then true, conspirator, that you are anxious for war? You shall have it ; villains, you shall have it. . . . You are crafty, astute, faithless, but more than all, you are cowards ; and to fight you we have steel, virtues, courage, the recollection of our victories, the irresistible ardor of liberty. And you, contemptible instruments of your masters' crimes, you who, in your delirium, dare to believe yourself powers, when you are but vile rep- tiles ; you who reproach us for having protected your property, for having carried far from your walls the horrors of war, and for saving the country ; you, in a word, who have made scorn, infamy, outrage, and death the lot of the defenders of the Republic tremble! From the Adige to the Rhine and the Seine is but a step ; tremble! Your iniquities are counted, and their reward is at the point of our bayonets."

Division Bernadotte: "The Republican constitution appears to be threatened. Our sensitive and generous souls are averse to believing it; but if the fact is true, speak! The same arms which assured national independence, the same chiefs who led the phalanxes, still exist. With such aid, you have but to wish it, to see the conspirators vanish from the picture of the living."

Division Sérurier : "Speak, citizen Directors, speak; and at once the wretches who polluted the soil of freedom will have ceased to exist. It will doubtless suffice to crush them, to summon some of our brave companions in arms from the armies of the Rhine and Moselle, and of Sambre and Meuse. We yearn to share with them the honor of purging France of its cruelest foes."

Division Joubert: "What! the odious Capet who for six years parades his shame from nation to nation, always pursued by our Republican phalanxes, would now bring them under the yoke! If this idea is revolting to any citizen whom love of country has once touched, how much more so to the old soldiers of the Republic!"

Division Baraguey d'Hilliers: "We renew the solemn oath of hatred to the factions, of war to the death to Royalists, of respect and fidelity to the Constitution of the Year III."

Division Delmas: "We have sworn to defend, to

the last drop of our blood, the liberty of our country. If it is possible that it should ever perish, we are determined to be buried beneath its ruins."

Division Victor: "No more indulgence, no more half-way measures! The Republic or death!"

The day after these addresses were signed by the officers and soldiers, Bonaparte wrote to the Direc- tory: "The soldier asks eagerly if, in reward for his toils and six years of war, he is to be assassinated in his hearthstone, at his return, — the fate which threatens every patriot. . . . Are there no more Republicans in France? After conquering Europe, shall we be forced to seek some little corner of the earth in which to end our sad lives? By one stroke you can save the Republic, and two hundred thousand lives which are bound with our fate, and secure peace within twenty-four hours: have the émigrés arrested, destroy the influence of the foreigners. If you need force, summon the armies. Demolish the presses in English pay, which are more sanguinary than ever Marat was. As for me, citizen Directors, it is im- possible for me to live amid such conflicting passions; if there is no way of putting an end to our country's sufferings, to crushing the assassinations and influ- ence of Louis XVIII., I present my resignation."

Bonaparte's soldiers looked upon him as a William Tell, a Brutus, the terror of tyrants, the saviour of liberty. Perhaps there was not a man in his whole army who suspected him of not being an ardent Re- publican. Yet, at that very moment, when he was,

so to speak, the inspiring spirit of the 18th Fructidor,
he was already, in intimate conversation, indicating
his plans of dictatorship and empire. In the Count
Miot de Mélito's Memoirs there is to be noticed a
very curious revelation: " I happened to be," he
says, "at Montebello with Bonaparte and Melzi, and
Bonaparte took us both a long walk in the vast gardens of this beautiful estate. Our walk lasted about
two hours, during which time the general talked
almost incessantly. ' What I have done so far,' he
said, ' is nothing. I am now only at the beginning
of my career. Do you think I have been triumphing
here in Italy for the greater glory of the lawyers of
the Directory? Do you think it was to establish
a republic! What an idea! A republic of thirty
million men! With our morals, our vices, is such a
thing possible? It is a chimera that fascinates the
French, but which will pass away like so many
others. What they need is glory, the gratification of
the vanity; but they know nothing of liberty. Look
at the army. The victories we have already won have
given the French soldier his real character. I am everything for him. Let the Directory think of deposing
me from my command, and we shall see who is master. The nation demands a man illustrious by reputation, and not for theories of government, phrases,
and the speeches of theorists, which the French don't
understand in the least. Give them a rattle, and
they are satisfied; they will amuse themselves with
it and let themselves be led, provided that one hides

the end towards which one leads them. . . . A party is moving in favor of the Bourbons. I do not mean to contribute to its triumph. I mean, some day, to weaken the Republican party ; but it shall be for my own advantage, and not for that of the old dynasty. Meanwhile, I shall keep in line with the Republican party.' "

He had to dissimulate for a few years more, and it was at the very moment that the young leader thus imprudently betrayed to Miot de Mélito his most secret thoughts, that he assumed this thoroughly Revolutionary aspect before the eyes of his army, and that by sending Augereau to Paris he prepared for the 18th Fructidor, — a day most fatal to the reactionary party, and full of the most direful results. We may say that in these circumstances, Bonaparte, who possessed all the Italian craft and astuteness, exhibited the skill and genius of a Machiavelli.

# XIII.

IN 1797 Bonaparte was a Republican, not, however, on account of the Republic but for his own advantage. What he condemned in the Royalists was not that they threatened the Republicans, but that they desired to bar his way to the throne. His indignation with the Royalist reaction was above all things the result of personal ambition. Apparently he was defending the Republic; in fact, he was laying the foundation of the Empire.

"I have been blamed," he said one day to Madame de Rémusat, "with having favored the 18th Fructidor; it is like blaming me for supporting the Revolution. It was necessary to get some profit from the Revolution, and not let all the blood be shed in vain. What! consent to surrender unconditionally to the House of Bourbon, who would have reproached us with all our misfortunes after their departure, and have silenced us by the desire we had shown for their return! Change our victorious flag for the white flag, which had not feared to mingle with the enemy's standard! And as for me, I was to be pacified with

a few millions and some duchy or other!—There
is one thing certain: I should have thoroughly
known how to dethrone the Bourbons a second time
if it had been necessary, and perhaps the best counsel
that could have been given them would have been to
get rid of me."

Bonaparte's double game never manifested itself
more clearly than in the preparations for the 18th
Fructidor. His official envoy to Paris, the man
whom he sent to the Directory as the official representative of the Republican feeling of his army, and
as the leader of the approaching *coup d'état*, was the
Jacobin general, the child of the Paris suburbs, Augereau. But at the same time he had sent on a recent
mission to the capital a man in whom he had perfect
confidence, — his aide-de-camp, Lavalette, whose manners and social relations were those of a man of the
old régime. Through Augereau, Bonaparte determined to act on the Republicans; through Lavalette,
on the Royalists. Already, in fact, he was plotting
the system of fusion which was to be the basis of his
domestic policy, and later to enable him to give the
titles of prince and duke to former members of the
Convention, and to endow regicides with the broad
ribbons of Austrian orders. Through Augereau, he
won the confidence of the most ardent democrats;
through Lavalette, he protected the families of the
émigrés and Josephine's old friends. His plan was
to secure for himself the benefits of the *coup d'état*,
and to appear to quell its excesses. By sending

Augereau to Paris he also derived this advantage, that he got rid of a general whose noisy Jacobin ways displeased him; for he so dreaded his influence as a demagogue that he wrote to Lavalette: "Augereau is going to Paris; don't confide in him; he has sown disorder in the army.  He is a factious man."

The Directory soon detected this double play, but it regarded Bonaparte as essential for its purposes, because his army would serve as a counterpoise to the ever-growing reactionary spirit, and it felt too weak to break with the conqueror of Italy.  Lavalette was equally an object of suspicion, and his goings and comings, his visits, his letters, and words, were all closely watched.  The antagonism between Bonaparte and Barras, although latent, was already visible to those who could look beneath the surface.  The Directory was about to win a victory which contained the seeds of defeat.  The 18th Fructidor was to produce the 18th Brumaire.

Madame de Staël, whose drawing-room was a centre of influence, was most eager in defence of the Republic and bitterly hostile to the reaction: she saw both Augereau and Lavalette.  "Although Bonaparte," she said, "was always talking about the Republic in his proclamations, careful observers discerned that it was in his eyes a means, not an end.  It was in this light that he regarded everybody and everything. The rumor ran that he wanted to make himself King of Lombardy.  One day I met General Augereau, who had just come from Italy, and was everywhere looked upon, and I think rightly, as an ardent Republican. I asked him if it was true that Bonaparte was thinking of making himself king. ' No, certainly not,' he answered; ' he's too well trained for such a thing.' This singular answer fitted well with the ideas of the moment. Earnest Republicans would have considered it a degrading thing that a man, however distinguished, should wish to use the Revolution for selfish purposes. Why was this view so shortlived among the French?" [1]

At this period Madame de Staël affected genuine adoration of Bonaparte. Lavalette met her at dinner at the house of M. de Talleyrand, the Minister of Foreign Affairs. "During the whole dinner," he says, "her praise of the conqueror of Italy had all the fire and exaggeration of inspiration. When we rose from table, we all went into a side room to see the hero's portrait, and as I drew back to let the others pass, she stopped, and said, ' What! should I think of going before an aide-de-camp of Bonaparte?' My confusion was so manifest that even she was a little embarrassed, and the master of the house laughed at her. I went to see her the next day; she received me so kindly that I often called on her afterwards."

Madame de Staël at that time nourished two passions: for Bonaparte and for the Republic. She, more than any one, urged on the *coup d'état* of Fructidor. "I am convinced," Lavalette says further,

---

[1] Madame de Staël's *Considerations upon the French Revolution.*

" that she had not foreseen the cruelties that would be inflicted on the defeated party, but I never saw such zeal in urging them." She herself was alarmed by the deed which her words had helped to bring about. She records that in the evening of the 17th Fructidor, the alarm was so great that most well-known persons left their houses for fear of arrest. In spite of her Republican zeal, she felt alarmed on account of relations with Royalists. One of her friends found a hiding-place for her in a little room overlooking the bridge Louis XVI.; there she passed the night, looking out on the preparations for the terrible events which were to take place a few hours later. Only soldiers were to be seen in the streets; all the citizens were indoors. The cannon which were massed about the building in which sat the Corps Législatif (the Palais Bourbon) rolled over the pavement; but, with that exception, absolute stillness prevailed. In the morning it was learned that General Augereau had led his troops into the Council of the Five Hundred, and there arrested the reactionary deputies. Two of the Directors were proscribed, and fifty-one representatives were driven in wagons through the agitated country, and sent, in iron cages, to deadly exile in Cayenne; the owners, editors, and writers of forty-one newspapers were likewise all transported; the elections of forty-eight deputies were cancelled; the press was gagged and silenced; the priests and émigrés were again driven out of the country: such were the consequences of

the 18th Fructidor; the triumph of the military spirit.
As Edgar Quinet says: "All respect for law was
lost; nothing was seen or admired but the drawn
sword. . . . After the victory of the soldiers, there
was nothing left to do but to crown a soldier."

It was Bonaparte who was to get all the profit from
the 18th Fructidor; but before the Royalists of Paris,
whom he was treating gently, with an eye to the
future, he wished to appear as disapproving of the
excesses of a day which was to be of so great service
to him. Lavalette wrote to him that he would tarnish his glory if he appeared to give his support
to unjustifiable assaults upon the national representatives and upon worthy citizens. These views made
so deep an impression upon Bonaparte that, during
the days that preceded the *coup d'état*, Bonaparte, in
his letters to the Directory, abstained from expressing
himself on the domestic affairs of France. Lavalette
had passed the evening of the 17th Fructidor at the
Luxembourg with Barras. From the ill-concealed
excitement of the Director's courtiers, he conjectured
what was in the wind, and went away early, determined not to make his appearance there the next
day, because he did not wish, by his presence, to
make it seem that Bonaparte approved of such violent measures.

Nevertheless, Lavalette went to see Barras the
next day but one. The Director said to him in a
very threatening way: " You have betrayed the Republic and your general. For more than six weeks

the government has received no private letters
from him: your opinion on recent events is well
known, and we do not doubt that you have painted
our conduct in the blackest colors; I want to tell
you that last evening the Directory seriously discussed the question whether you should not share
the fate of the conspirators who are on their way to
Guiana. Out of regard for General Bonaparte, you
remain at large; but I have this moment sent my
secretary to enlighten him on what has taken place
and on your conduct."

Lavalette replied with perfect coolness: " You are
quite mistaken; I have betrayed no one. The 18th
is a calamity; I can never be convinced that the
government has the right to punish blindly the representatives of the people, to break every law. For
six weeks I have written nothing else; and if you
wish to convince yourself of this fact, here is the key
of my desk; you may seize my papers." Lavalette
lingered a few days in Paris, lest his hasty departure
should be ascribed to fear. Before starting, he visited
General Augereau, to see if he could do anything for
him. The general spoke about Bonaparte with great
indifference, and about the 18th Fructidor with
much more enthusiasm than he would have shown
about the battle of Arcole. " Do you know," he
said, " that you ought to have been shot for your
conduct? But don't be alarmed; you may count on
me." Lavalette smiled, and thanked him; but he
saw that it was useless to put this kindness to the

test, and the next day he left for Italy. He left Paris the 1st Vendémiaire, when the Directory, the ministers, and all the constituted authorities were proceeding to the Champ de Mars to celebrate the first day of the Year VI. of the Republic.

For his part, Bonaparte, who posed before his army, which was entirely made up of Republicans, as an ardent supporter of the 18th Fructidor, had addressed the following proclamation to his troops: "Soldiers, we are about to celebrate the 1st Vendémiaire, a date most dear to the French; it will be a day of renown in the world's annals. This is the day from which dates the foundation of the great nation; and the great nation is called by fate to astonish and console the world. Soldiers, far from your country, and triumphant over Europe, chains had been prepared for you; you knew it, you spoke of it; the people awoke and seized the traitors; they are already in irons. You will learn, from the proclamation of the Executive Directory, the plots of the special enemies of the soldiers, and particularly of the divisions of the Army of Italy. This preference does us honor; hatred of traitors, tyrants, and slaves will be in history our proudest title to glory and immortality."

It was not Bonaparte alone who thus played the part of the fanatical Republican: there was Talleyrand, too, the former bishop, — Talleyrand who, some years later, at the Vienna Congress, was to speak of legitimacy with so much fervor. He wrote to Bonaparte four days after the 18th Fructidor: "A real conspiracy, and wholly to the profit of Royalty, had long been plotting against the Constitution. Already it had cast off its mask, and had become visible to the most indifferent eyes. The name of patriot had become an insult; every Republican institution was insulted; the bitterest foes of France had returned to it, and had been welcomed and honored. A hypocritical fanaticism had suddenly carried us back to the sixteenth century. . . . The first day speedy death was decreed for any one who should recall Royalty, the Constitution of '93, or the d'Orléans."

When Lavalette got back from Paris, he found Bonaparte installed at Passeriano, and he gave the fullest details of everything that had happened. The general asked, "Why, with such scornful processes, so much weakness? Then why such rashness, when boldness was enough? It was a piece of cowardice not to try Pichegru; his treason was flagrant, and the evidence was more than enough to condemn him. . . . Force is very well when one can use nothing else; but when one is master, justice is better." Then he continued his walk in the garden in silence. Finally, he added, as he took leave of Lavalette, "On the whole, this revolution will prove a good spur to the nation." In fact, the real conqueror of the 18th Fructidor was not the Directory; it was Bonaparte.

# XIV.

TOWARDS the middle of September, **1797,**
Bonaparte, accompanied by his wife, — his family had left after Pauline's marriage with General
Leclerc, — had taken up his quarters in the Friuli,
at the castle of Passeriano, there to conclude diplomatic negotiations with the Austrian government.
This was a fine country-place belonging to Manin, the
former doge, and was on the left bank of the Tagliamento, four leagues from Udine, and three from
the ruins of Aquileia. Here the warrior appeared as
a peace-maker. Being secured against the Royalists
by the *coup d'état* of the 18th Fructidor, from which
he got the profit without the odium, he at once
appeared in the light of a conservative, and in his
relations with the Austrian plenipotentiaries he remembered with pleasure that his wife was of high
rank and that he himself was a gentleman. He
already manifested his pretensions to noble birth of
which Prince Metternich speaks in his Memoirs.
According to the famous Austrian diplomatist, he set
great store by his nobility and the antiquity of his

family. "More than once," adds Prince Metternich, "he has tried to prove to me that only envy and calumny have been able to throw any doubts on his nobility. 'I am in a singular position,' he used to say. 'There are genealogists who trace my family back to the deluge, and others say that I am of low birth. The truth lies between the two. The Bonapartes are good Corsican gentlemen, not famous, because we have seldom left the island, and a good deal better than many of the coxcombs who presume to look down on us.'"

The Austrian plenipotentiaries were Count Louis de Cobenzl, the Marquis of Gallo, General Count Mersfeld, and M. de Ficquelmont. Count Cobenzl was at that time leading Austrian diplomatist. He had been ambassador to the principal European courts, and for a long time in Russia, during the reign of Catherine the Great, whose especial esteem he had succeeded in winning. "Proud of his rank and importance," we read in the *Memorial of Saint Helena*, "he had not a doubt that his manners and familiarity with courts would easily overwhelm a general who had risen from the camps of the Revolution; consequently he met the French general with a certain levity, but the air and the first remarks with which he was greeted soon put him in his proper place, in which he remained ever after." M. de Cobenzl was an accomplished man of the world, a true representative of the old régime. He was a brilliant and witty talker, who told most cleverly stories of every court of Europe; he was famous for his social skill, and he greatly amused Madame Bonaparte, who found in him the manners of the old court of Versailles.

The Marquis of Gallo, a most acute, supple, and conciliating man, was not an Austrian; he was a Neapolitan, and ambassador from Naples to the court of Vienna. There he had won such regard that Austria chose him for one of its plenipotentiaries.

"Yours is not a German name," Bonaparte said to him the first time he saw him. "You are right," answered the Marquis of Gallo; "I am ambassador from Naples." "And since when," asked the French general dryly, "have I had to treat with Naples? We are at peace. Has not the Emperor of Austria any more negotiators of the old stamp? Is all the old Viennese aristocracy extinct?" The Marquis, who feared lest these remarks should come to the official notice of the Vienna cabinet, at once devoted himself to smoothing down Bonaparte, who at once became gentle, being perfectly satisfied with having got an advantage over the Marquis which he never lost. The Marquis of Gallo, who later was ambassador from the Bourbons of Naples to the First Consul, then ambassador from King Joseph Bonaparte to the Emperor Napoleon, confessed to him frankly, when speaking of their first meeting, that no one had ever in his life so frightened him.

The two other plenipotentiaries were General von Mersfeld, a distinguished officer, an upright man, of fine manners, and M. de Ficquelmont, who was thoroughly versed in all the Austrian statecraft. Their meetings were held at Bonaparte's headquarters at Passeriano, and at the residence of the Austrian plenipotentiaries, at Udine, alternately. The negotiators took turns in dining at each other's houses. Distractions were fewer than at Montebello, but life there was not wholly without charm. "Our stay at Passeriano," says the Duke of Ragusa, "comes back most pleasantly to my memory; it had a quality that was nowhere repeated. . . . We devoted ourselves to active exercise, to maintain our strength and develop our skill; yet we did not neglect study and the cultivation of our mind. Monge and Berthollet used to teach us every evening; Monge giving us lessons in that science of which he established the principles, now so well known, — descriptive geometry."

It was at Passeriano that General Desaix visited Bonaparte. They spent several days together, and became much attached to each other. "Desaix," adds the Duke of Ragusa, "had not forgotten my prophecies, so quickly realized, about General Bonaparte; he reminded me of them as soon as he saw me. He expressed to General Bonaparte his desire to accompany him on his next campaign. It was from this visit that dates the first thought of the campaign in Egypt. Bonaparte liked to talk about this classic land; his mind was full of memories of history, and he took great pleasure in forming more or less feasible plans about the East."

Bonaparte's aides-de-camp found a peaceful pleasure in this agreeable stay at Passeriano; but the general had most serious matters to fill his mind, and his relations with the Directory, whose servant after all he was, became every day more strained. He regarded it a special token of their distrust that Bottot, the private secretary of Barras, had been sent to Passeriano. At table he loudly and frankly, before twenty or thirty persons, used to accuse the government of injustice and ingratitude. He suspected the Directors of trying to make use of Augereau as a rival, and with similar craft and subtlety he kept writing and saying that his health and energy were destroyed; that he needed a few years' rest; that he was unable to get on a horse; but that nevertheless the prosperity and liberty of his country always excited his liveliest interest. What would he have done if the Directory had taken him at his word?

With regard to diplomatic questions his opinions differed fundamentally from those of the government. He was convinced that peace was possible only on the condition of sacrificing Venice to Austria. The Directory, on the other hand, considering that the French Republic could not without dishonor abandon a republic to a monarch, desired not only Venetian independence, but that the whole peninsula should be made republican, that the temporal power of the Pope should be broken, and the kingdoms of Piedmont and Naples destroyed. This radical policy in no way suited Bonaparte's views. He knew that in order to attain supreme power he should need the clergy; and although he had so often declaimed against tyrants, he thought it better to show some consideration for the sovereigns whom within a few years he should have to treat as brothers. The attitude which he adopted at Passeriano bespeaks such calculations. A clear-sighted observer might have already detected, in this tool of the Directory, the First Consul and Emperor. By his education, his tastes, his marriage, his ideas and principles, he belonged to both the old society and the Revolution. From each he took what aid he could, for the gratification of his ambition and the realization of his dreams. " My campaign was not a bad one," he said one day to Madame de Rémusat, speaking of this period of his life. " I became an important person for Europe. On one hand, by means of my order of the day, I encouraged the Revolutionary system ; on the other, I secretly won the émigrés; I let them form hopes. It's always easy to deceive that party, because they never think of what is, but of what they want. I received most magnificent offers if only I would follow General Monk's example. The Pretender wrote to me, in his hesitating, flowery style. I secured the Pope more by not going to Rome than if I had burned his capital. Finally, I became important and formidable ; yet the Directory, which was uneasy about me, could bring no charge against me."

Never was the skilful dissimulation, which was one

of the principal qualities of Bonaparte's character, more ingenious and more refined. He wrote to the Directory: " My moral condition requires that I mingle with the mass of citizens. A great power has too long been entrusted to my hands. In every case I have employed it for the good of my country: so much the worse for those who, believing in no virtue, may have suspected mine. My reward is my own conscience and the verdict of posterity." October 1, 1797, he wrote to Talleyrand: " All that I am now doing, all the arrangements I am now settling are the last service I can render my country. My health is wholly destroyed; health is indispensable, and, in war, nothing can take its place. The government will doubtless, in accordance with my request of a week ago, have appointed a commission of publicists to organize a free Italy; new plenipotentiaries to continue or renew the negotiations; and, finally, a general to whom it can entrust the command of the army, for I know no one who can take my place in these three equally interesting posts."

The Directory was jealous and suspicious; it already had a presentiment that it would find its master in Bonaparte; but it rivalled him in dissimulation, and, in refusing to accept his resignation, made protestations of friendship which were anything but sincere. Bottot, Barras's secretary, wrote to Bonaparte, after his return from Passeriano to Paris, that his last moments at Passeriano had sorely distressed his heart: that cruel thoughts had accompanied him to the very doors of the Directory; but that these cruel thoughts had been dispelled by seeing the admiration and affection which the Directors felt for the conqueror of Italy. In spite of these protestations, which on both sides were mere political manœuvring, the hostility between Barras and Bonaparte, although lessened by Josephine's secret influence, was yet plain to clear-sighted eyes, and was to cease only with the act of violence of the 18th Brumaire.

# XV.

WHILE Bonaparte was at Passeriano, Josephine went to spend a few days at Venice, which had been occupied by a French garrison since May 16. Its old aristocracy had been overthrown, and a lawyer, Dandolo, had put himself at the head of the provisional government. Bergamo, Brescia, Padua, Vicenza, Bassano, Udine, were all separate republics. Everywhere were adopted the principles of the French Revolution; the Italian national colors were adopted, a confederation was formed. The proud Venetian Republic hoped to preserve its independence, but it was not without a secret uneasiness as to the negotiations at Passeriano. Its former attitude of haughtiness and hostility to Bonaparte and the French had become one of obsequiousness and entreaty. It besought the young conqueror to visit it, and promised him the most unheard-of ovations; but Bonaparte had already decided to abandon Venice to Austria in return for Mantua and the Adige, and he did not dare to show himself in a city which his plans were about to ruin. He clearly perceived

that after the ultra-democratic proclamations which
he had written, after the solemn sending to Paris of
busts of Junius and Marcus Brutus, he would appear
very inconsistent if he were to give over a republic,
bound hand and foot, to an emperor. If he had gone
to receive on the square of Saint Mark the applause
which the expiring city promised him, he would seem
to have played a traitor's part. His spirit of dissimulation did not go so far as that; but Josephine, who
was not admitted to diplomatic secrets, might go to
the Venetian festivities as to a simple pleasure-party.
She was averse to leaving Italy without seeing this
wonderful and famous city, and she got her husband's
leave to go there under the escort of Marmont. She
appeared at the City of the Doges, with all her usual
grace, kindliness, and amiability. "To see her so
affable and so smiling towards every class of society,
no one would have suspected the dark plans which her
husband was weaving against the independence of
the noble and illustrious Republic. Doubtless Venice
was at fault: its neutrality had been neither prudent
nor loyal; the Veronese Vespers had been a grave
crime. But the punishment was terrible, and what
would be the feelings of the patriots who were soon
to see that most terrible sight, — the annihilation of
their country?"

Yet Venice was still rejoicing; the credulous
populace still nourished illusions; so easy is it to
believe what one hopes. The nobility of the main-
land, with its long-lived jealousy of the aristocracy

of the lagoons, saw with pleasure the fall of the
oligarchy which it detested. The middle classes,
fancying themselves emancipated, noisily welcomed
the triumph of French ideas. As to the rabble, they
thought no more of the past, and scarcely considered
the future; delighted with the festivities, they gave
themselves up to the pleasures awaiting them with
true southern enthusiasm.

The Venetians, with the best will in the world,
being unable to prostrate themselves before the man
who held their fate in his hands, spared no pains at
the reception of his wife, to devise what could grat-
ify and flatter her. Madame Bonaparte spent four
days at Venice; it was one perpetual magical en-
chantment. The City of the Doges is most beautiful
with its wealth of marble palaces and magnificent
monuments, its pictures and frescoes, the masterpieces of Tintoretto, Titian, the two Palmas, Paul
Veronese, with its Piazza of Saint Mark, its wonderful cathedral, its Ducal Palace, rich in treasures
and memories! The visitor is overwhelmed with
admiration and respect when he enters the celebrated Greater Council Chamber, which in its wonderful pictures condenses the history of the Queen
of the Adriatic just as the grand gallery of Versailles
records the history of the Sun King! Here one
sees popes come to seek shelter in Venice, emperors
entreating its alliance, accepting its mediation; one
sees its fleets conquering islands, its armies scaling
ramparts, its victories on land and sea, and in the

middle of the ceiling, the Republic, in the form of a radiant woman, smiling at the display of its wealth and grandeur; then there is the series of the portraits of all the doges, from the first, Luca Anafeste, elected in 697, to the last, Manini, who, eleven hundred years afterwards, had just been deposed by the French! A singular omen: the portrait of the Doge Manini filled the only place left empty at the time of his election: there was no room for a successor. But the Venetians did not trouble themselves about this gloomy sign; they had but one care, — to give Madame Bonaparte a grand reception.

The first day the Grand Canal was in gala dress. A hundred and fifty thousand spectators filled the windows and roofs that overlooked it. There were boat-races; five or six long and narrow boats, propelled by but one man, contended over the course which ran from the beginning of the canal to the Rialto. The second day, a trip in the boats; all the gondolas were covered with flowers and garlands. The third day, another excursion, but by night, when palaces, houses, gondolas, were all illuminated: it was like a sea of flame; fireworks of many colors were reflected in the water, and the evening closed with a ball in the Ducal Palace. "If one reflects," says Marmont, "of the advantages which its situation gives to Venice, of the beauty of its architecture, of the endless movement of crowded boats, which make it look like a moving city, if one thinks of the efforts such circumstances called forth in this imaginative people with their exquisite taste and unbounded love of pleasure, one may conjecture the spectacle that was offered us. It was not Venice, the seat of power, but Venice, the house of beauty and pleasure."

No, it was no longer Venice in its power, — "Venice," as Chateaubriand says, "the wife of the Adriatic and Queen of the Seas, the Venice which gave emperors to Constantinople and kings to Cyprus, princes to Dalmatia, to the Peloponnesus, to Crete: the Venice which humiliated the Cæsars of Germany; the Venice of which monarchs esteemed it an honor to be the citizens; the Venice which, republican in the midst of feudal Europe, served as a buckler to Christianity; the Venice, planter of lions, whose doges were scholars, whose merchants, knights; the Venice which brought back from Greece conquered turbans or recovered masterpieces; the Venice which triumphed by its splendor, its courtesans, and its arts, as well as by its great men; Venice, at once Corinth, Athens, and Carthage, adorning its head with rostral crowns and diadems of flowers." No, it was no longer the former Venice. A profound decadence was visible in these festivities given in honor of Madame Bonaparte. What had become of that freest of cities which had maintained its independence since its foundation in the fifth century? Where were the famous bronze horses that had pawed the air above the entrance of Saint Mark's? They had been sent to Paris as part of the spoils. And the famous lion, the lion of the holy patron of Venice? He had suffered the same fate. The great saint whose relics are in the church founded in the beginning of the ninth century by the liberality of Justinian Participazio no longer protected the city which had so trusted in him. Ah ! what had become of her who

> " looks a sea Cybele, fresh from ocean,
> Rising with her tiara of proud towers
> At airy distance, with majestic motion,
> A ruler of the waters and their powers :
> *    *    *    *    *    *    *
> In youth she was all glory, — a new Tyre, —
> Her very byword sprung from victory,
> The ' Planter of the Lion,' which through fire
> And blood she bore o'er subject earth and sea;
> Though making many slaves, herself still free,
> And Europe's bulwark 'gainst the Ottomite.
> Witness Troy's rival, Candia ! Vouch it, ye
> Immortal waves that saw Lepanto's fight!
> For ye are names no time nor tyranny can blight."
>                         — *Childe Harold*, Canto IV.

It is all over; no more shall be seen the wedding of the doges and the Adriatic ! And where is the *Bucentaur*, the famous barge resembling Cleopatra's, the huge carved boat, with golden rigging? Where is the time when the Doge put forth from Venice in the *Bucentaur*, and, proceeding in triumph to the passage of the Lido, cast into the sea a consecrated ring, uttering these sacramental words: " *Desponsamus te, mare, in signum veri perpetuique dominii*,"— "Sea, we marry you in sign of true and everlasting dominion ! " The ambassadors of every power, even the Pope's nuncio, seemed by their presence to recognize the validity of this mystical marriage. What has become of the *Bucentaur?* At first it had been intended to send it to France in tow of some frigate; but for fear lest it should be captured on the way by some English cruiser, it was decided to burn it. Also there was burned that famous Book of Gold, in which patricians, even monarchs themselves, were proud to have their names inscribed. Venice, instead of rejoicing, had better have put on sackcloth, and the flowers with which it decked itself in its folly would have been better thrown on the coffin of its independence and glory! Its cries of joy seemed sounds of irony. The song of the gondoliers should have been a funeral wail. The authority which presided over its festivities was not a majestic and formidable doge, but a foreigner, a creole woman, who must have been surprised to appear amid the lagoons like a real queen.

# XVI.

## CAMPO FORMIO.

THE diplomatic negotiations still went on, but the time was coming near when they would have to be brought to some settlement or to be broken off. Bonaparte's situation, in spite of wonderful victories, continued to be critical. He was acting in a sense opposed to the orders of his government, and could only succeed by imposing his will upon it. At any moment there might arrive a messenger from Paris with a despatch that would at once overthrow the scaffolding he had so carefully constructed. He had more fear of the Directory than of Austria, and it was from the Luxembourg that came his principal difficulties. Bonaparte was about to send a double ultimatum, one for the Austrian government, the other for his own. By his private letters he had prepared Talleyrand, the Minister of Foreign Affairs, for the settlement on which he had already determined, and foreseeing the agreement which was to exist between himself and this once great lord, he had assumed in his communications airs of sympathy and confidence. In this correspondence he made short work of the Italian forces and of the revolutionary propaganda. He said : "I have no Italians in my army, except about fifteen hundred vagabonds picked up in the streets of the different cities. They are thievish, good-for-nothing fellows. . . . You imagine that liberty produces great results from a weak, superstitious people. . . . The King of Sardinia, with a battalion and a squadron, is stronger than all the Cisalpine people together. That is a historic fact. All that is only fit to put into proclamations and printed speeches is mere romantic stuff. . . . If we were to happen to adopt the external policy of 1793, we should make all the greater mistake because we have done well with the opposite policy, and we no longer have those great masses to recruit from, or that first outburst of enthusiasm which lasts but a short time." Being anxious to sacrifice the Venetians, he wrote, "They are a feeble, effeminately cowardly race, without land or water, of whom we have no need."

At this very moment he received from the Directory an order to revolutionize all Italy. This was the ruin of his plan, because he was anxious to maintain the Papal States, the kingdoms of Naples and Sardinia, and to give up Venice to Austria, while the Directory desired not only to save the Venetian Republic, but also to transform all the Italian States without exception into republics. The divergence of their views was complete. No one but Bonaparte would have dared to act in opposition to the letters and spirit of the government's instructions, but already he depended only on himself. Paying no attention to the Directory, he followed only his own inspirations, and, October 16, he had an interview with the four plenipotentiaries, which was destined to be decisive. Count Cobenzl announced that Austria would never renounce Mayence except in exchange for Mantua. Bonaparte, however, was determined that Mantua should remain in the Cisalpine Republic. A violent scene resulted from disagreement. Bonaparte arose in a fury, and stamping on the ground, exclaimed, "You want war; well, you shall have it!" And seizing a magnificent porcelain teaset which M. de Cobenzl used to boast every day that Catherine the Great had given him, dashed it with all his might upon the floor, shivering it into a thousand fragments. "See!" he shouted again; "such, I promise you, shall be your Austrian monarchy before three months are over!" Then he rushed out of the room.

Bonaparte was playing everything on one throw; he had smashed Count Cobenzl's porcelain, but was it so sure, if the Count had taken him at his word and the negotiations had been broken off, that he would have destroyed the Austrian monarchy so easily as he said? Was it certain that he would not be disavowed by the Directory? Would Paris have pardoned him for sacrificing Venice and refusing to revolutionize all Italy? Did he not run the risk of receiving that same evening a despatch which would upset his whole work? As on the battle-field, he adopted the boldest plan, and with no fear of the consequences that might ensue from his simulated wrath, he hastened the final result. A secret presentiment told him that he would overcome every obstacle, whether on the part of Austria or of the Directory, and that events would take the course he desired; that he was the master. And, in fact, everything conspired to further his plans. He was enjoying one of those runs of luck when the gambler suddenly wins everything and is amazed at his own good fortune. He knew very well that if the treaty were once signed, the Directory would not dare to refuse its ratification. As he rushed from the room, he in a loud voice ordered word to be sent to the Archduke Charles that hostilities would be resumed in twenty-four hours, and sprang into his carriage without seeming to notice the entreating gestures of the Marquis of Gallo, who, with many low bows, was begging him not to depart.

The next day the scene had changed. M. Cobenzl, on second thoughts, decided to accede to Bonaparte's proposition; and the French general, for his part, tried his best, by the utmost amicability, to secure a pardon for his pretended wrath of the day before. That same day (October 17, 1797) was signed the peace which took its name from the village of Campo Formio, which lies half-way between Udine and Passeriano. "Yet," says the Duke of Ragusa in his Memoirs, "not a single conference had been held there; it was merely the place where the treaty was signed. I was despatched thither to make the necessary preparations, and at the same time to invite the plenipotentiaries to push on to Passeriano, to which they very graciously assented. They signed before dinner, dating the treaty at Campo Formio, where the preparations had been made for form's sake; and doubtless there are still shown in this village the room in which the great event took place and the pen and table that were used. It is with these relics as with so many others." The copying of the treaties took all day; there were no more discussions. General Bonaparte was full of a charming gaiety, and, remaining in the drawing-room, he asked that no candles be brought when it became dark. They amused themselves with conversation and even with ghost stories, as if they were all staying together in some old castle. At last, towards ten o'clock, word was brought that the copies were finished. Bonaparte signed gaily. At midnight General Berthier was on his way to Paris with a copy of the treaty. Twelve hours later a messenger from the Directory reached Passeriano, bearing positive orders which would have prevented Bonaparte from signing the treaty if he had received them the evening before.

He felt anxious about the ratification. Would the Directory consent to the destruction of the Venetian Republic? Would the provisory government of Venice make one final effort to save the independence of the country? It commissioned three dele-

gates, one of whom was the lawyer Dandolo, to go
to Paris and spend whatever money was necessary to
prevent the ratification of the treaty. The Duke of
Ragusa remarks that this step, if it had succeeded,
would have been the ruin of Bonaparte, the tomb of
his glory; he would have been denounced to France
and to Europe, as having exceeded his powers and
as having, through corrupt means, shamefully abandoned a people and enslaved a republic. He would
have disappeared forever from the scene in the
deepest disgrace. Consequently, as soon as he
learned of the departure of the Venetian delegates
for France, his only thought was to have them arrested on the way. Duroc, who was sent in pursuit
of them, seized them and brought them to Milan,
where Bonaparte was. "I was in the room of the
commander-in-chief," Marmont continues, "when he
received them; the violence of his remarks may be
readily conjectured. They listened with quiet dignity; and when he had finished, Dandolo replied.
Dandolo, who generally possessed no courage, was
on that day filled with it by the greatness of his
cause. He spoke easily, and was indeed eloquent.
He enlarged upon the benefits of independence and
liberty, on what a good citizen owes to his country.
The force of his reasoning, his sincerity, his deep
emotion, brought tears to Bonaparte's eyes. He made
no reply, but dismissed the deputies most gently and
kindly; and ever since he has felt for Dandolo a constant kindness and fondness. He has always sought

for an opportunity to advance and benefit him; and yet Dandolo was a very ordinary man: but this man had stirred his heart by his lofty sentiments, and the impression he made has never faded."

In spite of the sorrow of the Directory, the Directory did not dare to refuse the ratification of a treaty which gave to France its natural boundaries, and recognized in Northern Italy the existence of a new republic founded on the principles of the French Revolution. "Peace at last," wrote Talleyrand, "and a peace such as Bonaparte desires! Receive my warmest congratulations, my dear General. Words fail me to describe everything that is felt at this time. The Directory is satisfied; the public delighted; everything is in the best condition. To be sure, we shall hear some lamentations from Italy; but that's nothing. Farewell, peacemaking General, farewell! friendship, respect, admiration, gratitude — there's no end to the list." France, always mercurial, at that moment was longing for peace as ardently as, a few weeks before, it had longed for war. Bonaparte had consulted his own interests at a most propitious moment, and yet every one was praising his disinterestedness. It was thought most admirable of him to renounce, out of patriotism, the game of battles for which his genius so well adapted him. He was compared to Cincinnatus returning to his plough; he was everywhere represented as a model of self-denial. The *Moniteur*, which doubtless was controlled by his friends, was preparing to make his return very

impressive. Everything was arranged for this purpose. The journey from Passeriano to Paris was to
inspire a host of stories to strike the imagination of
the masses and arouse public curiosity. Letters full
of the minutest details of this triumphal progress
appeared in swift abundance in the *Moniteur*, adding
to the extreme interest which was felt in the slightest
actions and most insignificant remarks of the conqueror of Italy. When he passed through Mantua,
he slept in the palace of the former dukes. In the
evening the whole city was illuminated. The next
day he reviewed the garrison; then he went to Saint
George, where there took place a military celebration
in memory of General Hoche, and at noon he embarked on a boat, to see the monument he had had
built in honor of the prince of Latin poets. He
parted from Josephine, who stayed some time longer
in Italy with her son Eugene; and November 17,
1797, left Milan for Rastadt, where a congress was
in session, destined to extend to the whole German
Empire the peace concluded between France and
Austria.

## XVII.

BONAPARTE left Milan November 17, 1797, accompanied by Marmont, Duroc, Lavalette, as well as by Bourrienne, his secretary, and Yvan, his physician. He passed through Piedmont, but refused to stop at Turin and see the King of Sardinia; but that monarch sent him his compliments and a number of presents, — two handsome horses with magnificent fittings, and two horse-pistols set with diamonds, which had belonged to the late King, Charles Emmanuel. Bonaparte crossed the Mount Cenis. When he reached Chambéry, he was greeted most warmly. Thence he went to Geneva, where he stopped for a day. He refused to call on Necker, who was waiting for him at the roadside, near the castle of Coppet. He also, in spite of the desires of his aides-de-camp, refused to visit Ferney, having a grudge against the memory of Voltaire. His carriage broke down a league from Morat, and he went part of the way on foot. The roads were filled by a vast crowd, who spent the night standing in order to see the conqueror of Italy. He reached Morat November 23; it was a market-day, and his arrival was most anxiously awaited: the chief magistrate prepared to receive him with all possible honors. Let us quote from a letter sent to Paris from Morat, and printed in the *Moniteur:* "I looked with keen interest and extreme admiration at this extraordinary man, who has done such great things, and seems to promise that his career is not yet concluded. I found him very like his portrait, — short, slight, pale, looking tired, but not ill, as I had heard. It seemed to me that he listened somewhat absent-mindedly and with no great interest, as if much more occupied with his own thoughts than with what was said to him. His face is full of intelligence, and wears an expression of constant reflection, revealing nothing of what is going on inside this thoughtful head, this sturdy nature, in which doubtless were forming plans destined to have great influence over the fate of Europe. A worthy citizen of Morat, about five feet seven or eight inches tall, was much struck by the general's appearance. 'That's a pretty small height for such a great man,' he exclaimed, loud enough to be heard by an aide-de-camp. 'It's exactly the height of Alexander,' I said, bringing a smile to the aide's face. He said, 'That is not the most striking point of resemblance.' Bonaparte stopped near the monument of bones at Morat and asked to be shown the place where the battle it commemorated was fought. They pointed out a plain in front of a chapel. An officer who had served in France explained how the Swiss, descending from the neighboring mountains, were able, aided by a dense wood, to outflank the Burgundian army and rout it. 'How large was this army?' asked Bonaparte. 'Sixty thousand men.' 'Sixty thousand men! They must have covered the mountains.' Then General Lannes said, 'Nowadays the French fight better than that.' 'At that time,' replied Bonaparte, 'the Burgundians were not Frenchmen.'"

The journey was a series of ovations. Reaching Berne at night, Bonaparte passed through a double line of brilliantly lit carriages, filled with pretty women. His entrance into Basle was announced by cannon on the city ramparts. At once the fortress of Huningue replied to the salvo of artillery. At Offenburg were the headquarters of Augereau, at that time commander-in-chief of the Army of the Rhine. Augereau was anxious to treat him as an equal; he sent an aide with his compliments to Bonaparte, and an invitation to stay a while with him. Bonaparte sent word that he was too busy to stop, and pushed on without seeing his former subordinate. He entered Rastadt under the escort of a squadron of Austrian hussars, and found there the plenipotentiaries of the German powers; but he did not care to tire himself in long and tedious negotiations, and was glad to be recalled by the Directory. He hastened to take post for Paris, and reached there December 5, at five o'clock in the afternoon.

Bonaparte went to the little house in the rue de la Chantereine whence he had departed, almost obscure,

twenty-one months before, and he returned famous.
The ambitious men who leave Paris, and are as
anxious about its judgment as was Alexander about
that of Athens, can never return thither without
anxiety. They wonder, and not without emotion,
what their glory will amount to in that vast city,
with its population so keenly susceptible, yet withal
so fickle, and where everything is soon lost in the
waves of that human ocean, the people. Great curiosity was excited by the return of the young conqueror. How would the Directors greet this hero
whose glory eclipsed their pallid renown? And what
did he want? To be a Cæsar? a Cromwell? a
Monk? a Washington? Such were the questions
that agitated the multitude; but the prevailing impression was that Bonaparte was one of Plutarch's
heroes, that his genius was only equalled by his self-
denial. The Parisians, in their eagerness to create
an idol, ascribed to their favorite every merit, every
virtue. The infatuation was universal; to see Bonaparte, to speak with him, became every one's ambition. The newspapers showed unvarying zeal in
printing the most trivial details about him. Every
other subject seemed insipid. Talleyrand called on
him the evening of ·his arrival. Bonaparte begged
to be excused from receiving him, and the next day
called at the Ministry of Foreign Affairs, where he
was received with marks of the warmest respect.
His interview with the Directors was most cordial.
Everywhere his affability and modesty were talked

about. Gratitude was felt for the visits he returned, not merely to the principal state functionaries, but also to humbler officials. In the *Moniteur* of December 10 we read: "General Bonaparte is living in his wife's house, rue Chantereine, Chaussée d'Antin. This house is simple, and with no pretence to luxury. It has been said that he will leave, on the 26th, for Rastadt. He goes out seldom, and unaccompanied, in a plain, two-horse carriage. He is often seen walking alone in his modest garden."

This little house in the rue Chantereine, which he had left, two days after his wedding, to go to Italy, and which recalled so many happy memories, was for him once more, to use Marmont's expression, the temple of love. But it was no fault of his brothers if he did not suffer there the torments of a keen jealousy.

We have said that he started from Milan November 17, leaving Josephine there, who meant to pass a few days there with her son, Eugene de Beauharnais, who had come from Rome to see her before her return to France. Lavalette says in his Memoirs, that Bonaparte's brothers, wishing to be the only ones who had any influence over him, tried to lessen that which Josephine possessed through her husband's love. "They tried," he goes on, "to arouse his jealousy; and for this purpose made the most of her stay at Milan, — a stay which was authorized by Bonaparte. His regard for his wife, his journeyings, his incessant preparations for the expedition to Egypt, gave him no time to indulge in such suspicions. I shall speak later about the intrigues of Bonaparte's brothers, and their determination to undermine Josephine in his heart. I was intimate with both, and thus fortunate enough to prevent, or much relieve, the mischief."

Bonaparte had scarcely time enough for jealousy; but, granting that he felt some pangs, the incessant gratification of his pride must have been an ample compensation. When he was at the theatre, no one listened to the actors; every glass was turned towards the box in which he half hid himself to make curiosity the keener. As soon as he went to walk, a crowd gathered about him. Knowing the Parisian character, and that the attention of the great capital would not long linger on the same subject, he did not make himself common, and in his language, as well as in his dress and manners, he affected a simplicity in marked contrast to his glory, which could not fail of its effect on a Republican public. In spite of this assumed modesty, he was perpetually devising methods of giving France and the world new surprises. At this time, it was not love, but ambition, that ruled his soul. Nevertheless, he continued to love Josephine; and although his affection had no longer the fire and flame of the first days of his married life, he must have regretted her absence at the triumphal festival of December 10 at the Luxembourg.

## XVIII.

THE festivity of December 10 took place at the Luxembourg, where the Directors were to give a formal reception to the conqueror of Italy. The rooms of the palace were too small for the occasion, so the large courtyard was turned into a vast hall adorned with trophies and flags. At eleven in the morning the members of the Directory assembled at the palace, at the rooms of their colleague, La Réveillère-Lepeaux. The ministers, the members of the Diplomatic Body, the officers of the garrison of Paris, were announced in succession. At noon the artillery posted in the garden gave the signal for the beginning of the festival. A band, playing the favorite airs of the French Republicans, preceded the procession, which passed through the galleries of the palace and went into the large courtyard. At the end, close to the main vestibule, rose the altar of the country, surmounted by statues of Liberty, Equality, and Peace. Below the altar were five chairs for the Directors, who wore a Roman dress, and a platform for the members of the Diplomatic Body. On

172

each side rose a vast semicircular amphitheatre for
the constituted authorities and the Conservatory of
Music. To the right and left of this amphitheatre
was a bundle of flags of the different armies of the
Republic. The walls were adorned with tricolored
hangings; and over the altar and the amphitheatre
was suspended a large awning. A vast multitude
filled the courtyard and the windows of the rooms,
which served as galleries. All the leaders of Parisian society were gathered at this entertainment,
which had been much talked about. Every one
looked eagerly forward to seeing and hearing the
man whose name was on every one's lips. The
women wore their handsomest dresses, anxious to
see and to be seen; they and the spectacle itself attracted equal attention. The men, proud of their
uniforms, the fashionable beauties, proud of their
splendor, were greeting one another; and the noisy
crowd awaited with impatience its favorite's arrival.
The President of the Directory gave orders to an
usher to go and summon the Ministers of War and
of Foreign Affairs, Generals Bonaparte and Joubert,
and the Chief of Brigade, Andréossy, who were in
the apartments of La Réveillère-Lepeaux.

The Conservatory orchestra played a symphony,
but suddenly the noise of the instruments was
drowned by an outburst of cheers. Cries arose from
every side, "Long live the Republic! Long live
Bonaparte! Long live the great nation!" "There
he is!" they shouted. "There he is, so young and so

famous! There is the hero of Lodi, of Castiglione, of Arcole, the peacemaker of the continent, the rival of Alexander and Cæsar! there he is!" His modest stature, his gauntness, his air of feebleness, made him no less majestic, for he wore the majesty of glory. No further attention was paid to the Directors or to the famous men who were there; on him, and on him alone, every eye was fixed. He advanced calmly and modestly, accompanied by the Ministers of Foreign Affairs and of War, and followed by his aides. The chorus of the Conservatory sang the Hymn to Liberty; the *Moniteur* tells us that " the assembly, in a transport of delight, repeated the chorus of the martial song. The invocation to Liberty and the sight of the liberator of Italy electrified every soul; the Directory, the whole procession, all who were there, arose and stood bareheaded during this solemn performance. General Bonaparte then advanced to the foot of the altar of the country, and was presented to the Directory by Citizen Talleyrand, Minister of Foreign Relations, who spoke as follows: 'Citizen Directors, I have the honor of presenting to the Executive Directory Citizen Bonaparte, who brings the ratification of the treaty of peace concluded with the Emperor. While bringing us this certain pledge of peace, he recalls, in spite of himself, the numberless marvels that have brought about this great event; but let him reassure himself, I will pass over in silence all that which will win the honor of history and the applause of posterity; I will

say to-day that this glory, which casts so bright a
glow on France, belongs to the Revolution. Without that, indeed, the genius of the Conqueror of
Italy would have languished in vulgar honors.'"
Talleyrand took great pains to combine the Republic
and the general in his eulogies. "All Frenchmen,"
he said, "have conquered in Bonaparte; his glory
is the property of all; there is no Republican who
cannot claim his portion. . . . Personal greatness,
so far from offending equality, is its proudest
triumph, and on this very day French Republicans
ought to feel themselves greater."

Citizen Talleyrand, as the future Prince of Bene-
vento was then called, used the language of the most
accomplished courtiers. Beneath democratic formulas
appeared the most refined and subtle tone of the old
régime. The ministers of Louis XIV. were not more
accomplished in the arts of flattery. Life is full of
curious vicissitudes! This Citizen Talleyrand, the
Minister of Foreign Affairs under the Republic one
and indivisible, was the former bishop who said mass
in the presence of Louis XVI. and Marie Antoinette
on the altar of the Champ de Mars, at the festival of
the Federation. This ardent Republican, the insti-
gator of the 18th Fructidor, was to appear one day
as the champion of legitimacy, and to forget that he
had ever been a minister of the Republic and of the
Empire.

Yet Bonaparte was extremely pleased by Talleyrand's delicate flatteries. Having been so often ac-

cused by the émigrés of being a mere Jacobin general,
he was highly gratified to be praised by a great nobleman, by one of the most important persons of the
former court. For his part, Talleyrand, who had a
keen appreciation of honors and wealth, knew very
well that this young man before whom he made obei-
sance would soon be in a position to distribute them;
hence the refinement in the flatteries which the former bishop addressed to his hero. "And when I
think," he said in closing, "of all that he has done
to make us pardon this glory, of the antique love of
simplicity that distinguishes him, of his love for the
abstract sciences, of the sublime Ossian who appears
to detach him from earth, when every one knows his
disdain for show, luxury, and splendor, those petty
ambitions of ordinary minds, then, far from dreading
his ambition, I feel that some day perhaps we may be
compelled to summon him from the calm joys of his
peaceful retreat. All France will be free, but he,
perhaps, never: such is his destiny. At this very
moment a new enemy calls him, renowned for its
hatred of the French and its insolent tyranny towards
all the nations of the earth. May it, through Bonaparte's genius, promptly expiate both, and may a
peace worthy of all the glory of the Republic be
imposed upon the tyrants of the sea; may it avenge
France and reassure the world!"

They scarcely listened to Talleyrand, and found
him long-winded; for they were impatient to hear
Bonaparte, the hero of the day. Every instant which

postponed the moment when the hero of Arcole was to speak seemed to them like time lost, and only the extravagant praise which he heaped upon the hero of the day excused the length of the Minister's speech. Citizen Talleyrand finished his peroration with these words: "Carried away by the pleasure of speaking about you, General, I perceive too late that the vast throng which surrounds you is impatient to hear you, and you, too, must blame me for delaying the pleasure you will have in listening to one who has the right of addressing you in the name of all France and of addressing you in the name of an old friendship."

At last Bonaparte was about to speak. His simple and modest countenance, said the *Moniteur*, contrasted with his great reputation. Every one imagined him commanding at the bridge of Lodi, at Arcole, at the crossing of the Tagliamento, or dictating peace at Campo Formio. There was a deep silence. Bonaparte handed to the President of the Directory the Emperor's ratification of the treaty of Campo Formio, and spoke as follows: "Citizens, the French people, in order to be free, had to fight with its kings. In order to attain a constitution founded on reason, it had to contend with eighteen centuries of prejudice. The Constitution of the Year III. was made, and you triumphed over every obstacle. Religion, feudality, royalty, have successively governed Europe for twenty centuries, but the peace you have just concluded dates the era of representative governments. You have succeeded in organizing the great nation whose vast territory is limited because nature itself has drawn its boundaries. You have done more. The two fairest parts of Europe, long since so famous for the arts and sciences, and for the great men whose birthplace it was, see with the greatest hopes the genius of liberty rising from the tomb of their ancestors. They are the two pedestals on which destiny is to erect two powerful nations. I have the honor to hand to you the treaty signed at Campo Formio and ratified by His Majesty the Emperor. This peace assures the liberty, the prosperity, and the glory of the Republic. When the happiness of the French people shall be established on better organic laws, all Europe will become free."

This short speech, delivered in a jerky voice, in a tone of command, produced a deeper impression than would have done the voice of the most famous orators of the century. When Bonaparte had finished, rapturous applause broke forth on every side, and spreading from the rooms, it continued all about in the neighboring streets, which were filled by a dense crowd.

Then Citizen Barras began to speak as President of the Directory, and it must be said that if, as generally asserted, he nourished a secret jealousy of Bonaparte, he was able to conceal it; for his speech was even more enthusiastic than Talleyrand's, as may be inferred from the opening words: "Citizen General, Nature, chary of prodigies, bestows seldom great

men upon the world, but it must be desirous to mark
the dawn of liberty by one of these phenomena, and
the sublime Revolution of the French people, without
precedent in the history of nations, has been permitted
to add a new genius to the list of great men. You,
first of all, Citizen General, have known no equal,
and by the same force with which you have shattered
the enemies of the Republic, you have surpassed all
the rivals that antiquity held up before you. . . .
After eighteen centuries, you have avenged France
for the fortune of Cæsar. He brought into our country subjection and destruction ; you have carried into
his ancient land liberty and life. Thus is paid the
huge debt which the Gauls had contracted to haughty
Rome." Bonaparte avenging Cæsar's good fortune
is, to say the least, a singular notion. Then Barras,
adopting a less austere tone, denounced " that herd
of intriguing, ambitious, ignorant, destructive men,
whose plans are destroyed, whose powerlessness is
unveiled, whose ill-gotten wealth is unmasked by
peace." Then he broke out against the cabinet of
London, " which, ignorant of the art of war, understands only how to mix poisons and to sharpen assas-
sins' daggers." After a long eulogy of the "immortal
18th Fructidor," Barras ended by inviting Bonaparte
to punish the British government. " Your heart," he
said, " is the Republican temple of honor ; it is to the
mighty genius which fills you that the Directory en-
trusts this grand enterprise. Let the conquerors of
the Po, the Rhine, and the Tiber follow in your foot-

steps; the ocean will be proud to carry them, for it is an unconquered slave who blushes at his chains; as it roars, it invokes the earth's wrath against the tyrant who burdens it with his fleets. It will fight for you; the elements second a free man. . . . You are the liberator whom outraged humanity summons with plaintive cries. . . . Of the enemy you will find only his crime. Crime alone sustains this perfidious government; crush it, and its fall will speedily teach the world that if the French people is the benefactor of Europe, it is also the avenger of the rights of nations."

After his long and pompous harangue, Barras held out his arms to Bonaparte and gave him a fraternal embrace. "All the spectators were moved," says the *Moniteur;* "all regretted that they, too, could not embrace the General who has deserved so well of his country, and offer him their share of the national gratitude."

Bonaparte then descended the steps of the altar, and the Minister of Foreign Relations led him to a chair set in front of the Diplomatic Body. Then the choruses and the orchestra of the Conservatory performed the *Song of the Return*, the words by Citizen Chénier, the music by Citizen Méhul. There was a couplet for warriors, one for old men, one for the bards, one for young girls. The song ended thus : —

"THE WARRIORS.

Let us unite in bonds of Hymen our hands and our hearts.

THE YOUNG GIRLS.
Hymen and love are the Conqueror's reward.

THE WARRIORS.
Let us create other warriors, and bequeath to them victory

THE WARRIORS AND THE YOUNG GIRLS.
That some day, at their words, their bright eyes,
One will say: They are the children of the brave!
That, deaf to tyrants, to slaves,
They always hearken to the voice of the oppressed."

The Minister of War then presented to the Directory General Joubert and Chief of Brigade Andréossy, whom Bonaparte had commissioned to take to the Directory the flag presented to this brave army, in token of the national gratitude, by the Legislative Body: it bore inscriptions in gold letters recounting the principal exploits of the conquerors of Italy. They formed most glorious record: that they had taken one hundred and fifty thousand prisoners, five hundred and fifty pieces of siege artillery, and six hundred field-pieces; that they had won eighteen pitched battles; that they had sent to Paris the masterpieces of Michael Angelo, Guercino, Titian, Paul Veronese, Correggio, Albano, the Carracci, Raphael, and Leonardo da Vinci! There was the famous standard, the oriflamme of the Republic! "What Frenchman," exclaimed the Minister of War, "what Frenchman worthy of the name will not feel his heart beat at the sight of this banner? Eternal monument of the triumph of our arms, be forever consecrated in the French capitol, amid the trophies won from conquered nations! Glory to you, valiant defenders of our country, generals and soldiers, who have covered with such glory the cradle of the Republic!"

After a speech from General Joubert and another from Andréossy, the artillery saluted the banner with a general salute. The President of the Directory received it from the hands of the two warriors. "In the name of the French Republic," he exclaimed, "I salute you, the flag recalling such mighty feats! . . . Brave soldiers, proceed to the banks of the Thames to rid the universe of the monsters who oppress and dishonor it. . . . Let Saint James's Palace be overthrown! The country wishes it; humanity requires it; your vengeance commands it. . . . Citizen General, you appear surrounded with the halo of your glory within the walls where, a few months ago, raving conspirators madly shouted, 'And this man still lives!' Yes, he lives for the glory of the nation and the defence of the country." The Conservatory choruses chanted the *Song of Return*, the public joining in, as a superior officer carried away reverentially the banner of the Army of Italy, to hang it aloft in the Council Room of the Directory.

It was a grand festivity; the transports of enthusiasm were sincere and generous. The government that presided over these solemn rites has been too often the subject of derision. Did it not possess one talisman to console every misfortune, — victory? Could it, in sight of the amazed and fascinated Diplomatic Body, give to France that fine, glorious name, of which the whole world judged it worthy, that of the great nation? Yes; it was with a sort of religious awe that this joyous multitude pronounced the word, liberty. Yes; on that day the Revolution appeared under an immortal aspect. Yes; the valiant soldiers who had wrought such miracles of heroism felt that at last they were amply rewarded for their fatigues, their sufferings, their triumphs. Doubtless it is easier to criticise than to imitate the Directory. A government which could use such haughty language in the face of Europe has claims, in spite of its faults and weaknesses, upon the indulgence of posterity. A government that gave to France its natural boundaries, and which could win not merely the territory, but also the hearts of the people it annexed, rested on principles and ideas of a grandeur that cannot fail to be recognized.

# XIX.

## AN ENTERTAINMENT AT THE MINISTRY OF FOREIGN RELATIONS.

IN his *Souvenirs of a Sexagenarian*, the poet Arnault narrates that in June, 1789, while walking near the Swiss lake, at Versailles, he noticed a man lying down under a tree, apparently plunged in solitary and philosophic thought. "His face, which was not devoid of charm," he goes on, "struck me less by its beauty than by its expression, by a certain combination of indifference and malignity, which gave it a very singular air, as if it were the head of an angel animated by the mind of a devil. It was evidently of a fashionable man, who was accustomed to arouse more interest in others than he felt for them; of a man who, though young, was already sated with worldly pleasures. I should have inclined to suppose it was the face of some favorite colonel, had not the cut of the hair and the bands told me that it belonged to an ecclesiastic, and the pastoral cross assured me that this ecclesiastic was a bishop."

A year later, July 14, 1790, among the half-million spectators who covered the slope of the Champ de

Mars was Arnault, watching the Festival of the Federation, when he saw on a hillock where mass was to be celebrated in the open air, a bishop advancing, a cope on his back, a mitre on his head, cross in hand, distributing floods of holy water with patriotic prodigality on the royal family, the court, the army, and the populace. "What was my surprise," he goes on, "to recognize in him the prelate of Versailles! For a year I had heard the Bishop of Autun much talked about. His face explained to me his conduct; and his conduct his face."

Arnault must have been still more surprised to find, in 1797, Monseigneur the Bishop of Autun transformed into Citizen Talleyrand, the Minister of Foreign Relations of the French Republic. Such a metamorphosis was without parallel; it was an avatar.

How many things had happened since the Festival of the Federation! On the day after the September massacres Talleyrand had obtained a passport for England, signed by all the ministers, on Danton's motion. From London he continued, it was said, to maintain relations with this terrible leader, which, however, did not prevent his being accused and inscribed on the list of émigrés at the end of 1792, on account of the discovery, in the celebrated iron wardrobe, of a letter in which he secretly offered his services to Louis XVI. In London he was generally regarded as a dangerous person; and early in 1794 the Alien Bill was applied to him. He set sail on a

Danish ship for the United States, and there awaited events.

After Robespierre's death he tried hard to get leave to return to France. His former vicar-general and acolyte at the mass of the Federation, Desrenaudes, solicited the favor of persons of influence. As M. Frédéric Masson has said in his remarkable book, *The Department of Foreign Affairs during the Revolution*, the exile reminded his former mistresses of his good fortunes; Danton's friends, of his relations with their chief; the stock-jobbers of old times, of the speculations which had made him their master. Legendre was for him, and Madame de Staël, and Boissy d'Anglas. Madame de la Bouchardie sang to Chénier the *Exile's Romanza*, and Chénier decided to support, before the Convention in the meeting of September 4, 1795, the petition which Talleyrand had sent from Philadelphia, soliciting permission to return to France. The Convention granted his request. He received a warm welcome in Paris on his return. Ladies who had formerly been leaders of fashion remembered his wit and his fine manners; their successors took him up out of curiosity. He became acquainted with one of the influential people of the day, Madame de Staël, who wanted him to be made a minister; but this, Carnot flatly opposed. "Don't let me hear a word about him," said the former member of the Committee of Public Safety. "He has sold his order, his king, his God. This Catelan of a priest will sell the whole Directory."

But Madame de Staël had more influence than Carnot; and the ex-Bishop of Autun was appointed Minister of Foreign Relations in July, 1797. His first thought, — for he had the gift of foresight, — was to secure the good graces of the man of the future, of the commander-in-chief of the Army of Italy. He wrote to him: "I have the honor of informing you, General, that the Executive Directory has just appointed me Minister of Foreign Relations. Naturally awed by the functions of which I feel the perilous importance, I need to reassure myself by reflecting what means and aids your glory brings to our negotiations. The mere name of Bonaparte is an ally able to remove every difficulty. I shall hasten to send to you all the views which the Directory shall charge me to transmit to you; and Fame, your ordinary means of communication, will often deprive me of the happiness of informing it of the manner in which you shall have carried them out."

When Bonaparte returned to Paris, Talleyrand was anxious to overreach him, to get possession of him, and determined to give a great entertainment in his honor, but he waited until Josephine should come. The former Viscountess of Beauharnais would well suit a place where met those of the old nobility who had come over more or less to the Revolution. Madame Bonaparte had a weakness for luxury, dress, and pleasure; in the drawing-room of the Minister of Foreign Relations she would feel herself in her element. Her grace and amiability would work wonders; she would modify the effect of her husband's rough, violent manners. She would recognize with emotion old friends who would hope to obtain honors and money through her influence. How delighted she would be to see arising again what she had thought forever lost, — the elegance, urbanity, the life of the drawing-room! Josephine reached Paris from Italy January 2, 1798. The ball of the Minister of Foreign Relations was set for the day following.

First a word about the ball-room. The ministry was a mansion of the Faubourg Saint Germain, the Hôtel Gallifet, a rich and costly dwelling, still unfinished in 1786, so that its former owners had had scarcely time to get settled in it. It was in the rue du Bac, at the corner of the rue de Grenelle, between a courtyard and a garden; the mansion on the side of the court being adorned by a great open peristyle, consisting of Ionic columns thirty feet high. To the left another peristyle with Doric columns forms a covered passage leading to the grand staircase. The façade towards the garden is adorned with Ionic columns; to the left is a gallery ninety feet long. Talleyrand prepared everything with a lavish hand. It was a magnificent ball: the grand staircase was covered with sweet-smelling plants, the musicians were placed in the cupola, decorated with arabesques, at the top of the staircase. All the walls of the drawing-rooms were painted over anew. A little Etruscan temple was built, in which was set the bust

of Brutus, — a present from General Bonaparte. In
the garden, which was illuminated by Bengal lights,
were tents in which were soldiers from all the different corps of the Paris garrison. At length the ball
began. The Minister did the honors with perfect
grace : he had altered his political opinions, but not
his manners. He was a Republican whose ways continued those of the Monarchy. He loved show and
splendor, and had the cold politeness, the repose of
good society, the indifference tinctured with malice,
the exquisite tact, the delicate perceptions, which
marked the men of the old régime. He brought into
a new world the manners of the Œil de Bœuf and
of the court of Versailles. This entertainment given
by a former bishop, in an aristocratic dwelling, which
had been made national property and turned into a
ministry, was a sign of the times. For many years
no show, pomp, and splendor had been seen. No one
would imagine himself in the city of revolutionary
dances, of red caps, of the scaffold. Perfumes took
the place of the smell of blood, and the sufferings and
perils of the past seemed but a bad dream. The
pretty women, the flowers, the lights, — one would
have thought the happy days of Marie Antoinette
had returned.

Madame Bonaparte was much impressed. She was
looked at a great deal, but her husband produced
infinitely more effect. The presence of the hero of
Arcole, the signer of the peace of Campo Formio,
was the great attraction of the evening. His un-

usual, strongly marked face, his Roman profile, his eagle eye, aroused much more admiration than did any of the fashionable beauties. A glance, a word, the slightest token of attention on his part, was regarded as a great favor.

As he entered the ball-room he said to the poet Arnault: "Give me your arm; I see a great many who are ready to charge on me; so long as we are together, they won't dare to break in on our talk. Let us walk about the hall; you will tell me who all the masks are, for you know everybody." There was a young girl approaching with her mother, *matre pulchra, filia pulchrior,* both dressed alike, in a dress of white crape, trimmed with two broad satin ribbons, and the edge bordered with a puff of the size of a thumb, in pink gauze worked with silver. Each wore a wreath of oak-leaves. The mother wore diamonds; the daughter, pearls : that was the only difference in their attire. The mother was Madame de Permont; the daughter, the future Duchess of Abrantès. The Turkish Ambassador, a favorite with all the ladies, to whom all the theatre proprietors had given numerous entertainments to make money and escape failure, the Turk whose popularity had waned before that of the conqueror of Italy, was most enthusiastic over the beauty of Madame de Permont, who was a Comnena. "I told him," murmured Bonaparte, "that you were a Greek."

Arnault, when the general had left his arm, sat down on a bench between two windows. Scarcely had he taken his place when Madame de Staël sat down beside him. "It's impossible to approach your General," she said; "you must present me to him." She grasped the poet and led him straight to Bonaparte through the crowd that drew back, or rather, that she pushed back. "Madame de Staël," said Arnault to the general, "declares that she needs some other introduction to you than her name, and asks me to present her to you. Allow me, General, to obey her." The crowd gathered about and listened with great attention. Madame de Staël first overwhelmed the hero with compliments, and after giving him clearly to understand that he was in her eyes the first of men, she asked him, "General, what woman do you love best?" "My wife," he answered. "That is very natural; but whom do you esteem the most?" "The one who is the best housekeeper." "I can understand that. But who do you think is the first of women?" "The one who has most children, Madame." The company burst out laughing; and Madame de Staël, much discomfited, said very low to Arnault, "Your great man is a very odd man."

At midnight the orchestra played the *Parting Song*, and all the women made their way to the gallery and sat down at a table with three hundred places. Talleyrand proposed toasts, each one being followed by couplets composed by Desprès and Despréaux, sung by Lays, Chenard, and Chéron. Between the songs, Dugazon told a comic story about a German baron, — a sort of entertainment much admired at that time.

After the supper the ball went on again. Bonaparte took leave at one in the morning. Throughout the supper he kept close to his wife, paying attention to her alone. According to Girardin he was not sorry to have it said that he was much in love with her and excessively jealous.

The ball cost 12,730 francs, without counting the singers, the supper, and the police. It was a large sum for a ball, but it was money well spent. From this investment the ex-B shop of Autun was to draw large profits. The entertainment of the Minister of Foreign Relations had been a union of the old and new society, a gracious and brilliant symbol of conciliation and fusion. Members of the Convention, regicides, Jacobins, had appeared there side by side with the great lords and ladies of other days. That is why it so pleased Bonaparte, who recalled it at Saint Helena, and said, "Minister Talleyrand's ball bore the stamp of good taste." It was indeed a political and social event, a real restoration; a restoration of the manners and elegance of the old régime; the beginning of a new court. From beneath the democratic mask of Citizen Talleyrand was already peering the face of the Lord High Chamberlain; and Bonaparte, knowing that under every form of government the French would love luxury and show, festivities and pleasure, honors and decorations, was doubtless already dreaming of the future splendors of the Tuileries.

## XX.

BONAPARTE appeared at the height of glory, and yet he was not contented. In vain the multitude worshipped him with something like idolatry: nothing could satiate his ambition. The *Moniteur* was filled with praise of him in prose and verse. There was this distich by Lebrun, surnamed the French Pindar: —

> " Hero, dear to Peace, the Arts, and Victory, —
> In two years he wins a thousand centuries of glory ! "

and this impromptu of an old man, Citizen Palissot, who in his own fashion thus reproduced the denunciation of Simeon: —

> " Over tyrants armed against us
> I have seen my country triumph.
> I have seen the hero of Italy —
> He chained to his knees
> With a triple knot of brass Discord and Envy.
>
>> " Fate, I scorn thy shears ;
>> After so glorious a sight
>> What does life still offer me ? "

No sovereign in his own capital has ever produced a greater impression than the hero of Arcole. His modest dwelling in the rue Chantereine was more famous than mighty palaces. One evening when he was going home he was surprised by finding workmen changing the sign bearing the name of the street, which henceforth was called rue de la Victoire. At the theatre it was in vain that he hid himself at the back of the box; he was, in spite of himself, the object of enthusiastic demonstrations. One morning he sent his secretary, Bourrienne, to a theatre manager to ask him to give that evening two very popular pieces, if such a thing were possible. The manager replied, "Nothing is impossible for General Bonaparte; he has struck that word out of the dictionary."

When he was elected a member of the Institute, December 26, 1797, he produced perhaps a greater effect in his coat embroidered with green palm-leaves than in his general's uniform. The day of his reception at the palace of the Louvre, where the meetings of the Institute were held at that time, the public had eyes only for this wonderful young man. Chénier happened to read that day a poem in commemoration of Hoche; but the hero of the occasion was not Hoche, but Bonaparte, and the passage which provoked the heartiest applause was one in which the poet spoke of a projected invasion of England. The whole company burst into cheers, and that evening Bonaparte received, among other

visits, that of Madame Tallien, who came to congratulate him on his new triumph. Josephine greatly
enjoyed her husband's glory, and nothing troubled
her happiness. Her son Eugene had returned from
Italy; her daughter Hortense, who was a pupil in
Madame Campan's boarding-school at Saint Germain,
seemed to share her brother's amiable and brilliant
qualities. In the month of March, 1798, this charming girl, whom Bonaparte loved as his own child,
acted before him, at her school, in *Esther*, recalling
thus the performances at Saint Cyr under Louis
XIV.

Josephine had never been happier; her brothers-in-
law, in spite of their dislike of her, had not been able
to make any trouble between her and her husband,
who then had neither time nor cause for jealousy.
She was very fond of society, and liked to see her
little house in the rue de la Victoire crowded with
all the principal people of Paris. She used to give
literary dinners there, when her husband's sparkling,
profound, and original conversation amazed such
students as Monge, Berthollet, Laplace; such writers
as Ducis, Legouvé, Lemercier, Bernardin de Saint-
Pierre; such artists as David and Méhul.

The *Moniteur* was untiring in its praise of the
universal genius of this young general, who called
forth the admiration of his colleagues of the Institute, who talked of mathematics with Lagrange; of
poetry, with Chénier; of law, with Daunou; and of
all, well. But Josephine's love, the circle of cour-

tiers who surrounded him, his universal success, the
perpetual gratifications of his pride which fortune
showered upon him, were all incapable of satisfying
his ardent, restless spirit, which imperatively demanded great emotions, great risks, great dangers.
Restless, and yearning for action, he uneasily waited
for the moment to come when the public should
grow tired of his glory as of everything else. "No
one remembers anything at Paris," he said to Bourrienne. "If I stay long without doing anything, I
am lost. One fame succeeds another in this great
Babylon; no one will look at me if I go three times
to the theatre, so I go very seldom." The administration of the Opera offered him a special performance, but he declined it. When Bourrienne sug-
gested that it would be a pleasant thing for him to
receive the applause of his fellow-citizens, "Bah!"
he replied, "the people would crowd about me just
as eagerly if I were going to the scaffold." "This
Paris weighs on me," he said on another occasion,
"like a coat of lead." In this city which swallows
so many reputations, and where everything so soon
grows old, he remembered Cæsar, who would have
preferred being first in a village to being second in
Rome. Doubtless there was in all France no name
so famous as his, but officially, the Directors were
above him; they were, in fact, the heads of the government of which he was but a subordinate. By a
simple official communication they could have deprived him of his command. The Duke of Ragusa

has justly remarked: "If Bonaparte, who was destined to have an easy success the 18th Brumaire,
had, early in 1798, made the slightest attempt against
the Directory, nine-tenths of the citizens would have
turned their back upon him." Madame de Staël tells
the story that one evening he was talking to Barras
of his ascendancy over the Italians, who wanted to
make him Duke of Milan and King of Italy. "But,"
he added, "I contemplate nothing of the sort in any
country." "You do well not to think of such a
thing in France," replied Barras; "for if the Directory were to send you to the Temple to-morrow, there
would not be four persons to object to it."

Bonaparte felt in his heart that Barras spoke the
truth. A capital like Paris seemed to him odious
unless he were its master. To have to depend on the
Directors, the Councils, the ministers, the newspapers,
was an intolerable weariness. For two years he had
been without superior control; he had acted like an
absolute monarch, and he felt out of his element in a
city where the reins of government were not in his
hands. At the end of January, 1798, he said: "Bourrienne, I don't want to stay here; there is nothing to
do. They won't listen to anything. I see very well
that if I stay, it will be all up with me very soon.
Everything wears out here; my glory is all gone;
this little Europe can't supply any. I must go to the
East; that's where all great reputations are made.
But first I want to visit the ports, to see for myself
what can be undertaken. I will take you, and

Lannes, and Sulkowski. If, as I fear, an invasion of England seems doubtful, the Army of England will become the Army of the East, and I shall go to Egypt."

Bonaparte's visit to the northern ports, which he began February 10, 1798, was of only a week's duration. He returned to Paris through Antwerp, Brussels, Lille, and Saint Quentin. "Well, General," asked Bourrienne, "what's the result of your trip? Are you satisfied? For my part, I must confess that I didn't find any great resources or grand hopes in what I saw and heard." Bonaparte replied: "The risk is too great; I sha'n't venture it. I don't want to trifle with the fate of France."

From that moment the expedition to Egypt was determined. The year before, at Passeriano, Bonaparte had said: "Europe is a mole-hill; you find great empires and great revolutions only in the East, where there are six hundred millions of men." To grow greater by remoteness; to win triumphs in the land of light, of the country of the founders of religions and of empires; to use the Pyramids as the pedestals of his glory; to attain strange, colossal, fabulous results; to make the Mediterranean a French lake; to traverse Africa and Asia; to wrest East India from England, — such were the vast dreams of this man who, with more reason than Fouquet, — for Fouquet had only money, and he had glory, — was tempted to exclaim, in a moment of rapture: " *Quo non ascendam?* "  " Whither shall I not rise ? "

The aim of the expedition he proposed to undertake was unknown, yet every one wanted to accompany him. No one knew where he was going, but he was followed blindly, for faith was felt in his star. Strangely enough, Bonaparte did not give any indications, even to his principal generals, of the point of destination. The *Moniteur*, in its issue of March 31, having had the imprudence to mention Egypt, the Directory nullified the effect of the blunder by publishing an order commanding General Bonaparte to go to Brest to take command of the Army of England.

Military men were not alone in asking to take part in this expedition: civilians, scholars, engineers, artists, also wished to go along. Bonaparte always regretted that he had not been able to take with him Ducis, the poet, Méhul, the composer, and Lays, the singer. But Ducis was too old to endure the hardships of a campaign, Méhul was bound to the Conservatory, and Lays to the Opera. "I am sorry that he won't go with us," said the general to Arnault, speaking of this singer; "he would have been our Ossian. We need one; we need a bard, who might, when the occasion arose, sing at the head of our columns. His voice would have had such a good effect on the soldiers. No one would suit me better than he." Bonaparte wished to transfer the civilization of Paris to the shores of the Nile. From the *savants* he chose Monge, Berthollet, Denon, Dolomieu; from the authors, Arnault and Parceval; from the artists, Rigel, the pianist, and Villeteau, the singer, who took Lays's parts at the Opera.

Bourrienne, who was in the secret of the expedition, asked the general how long he meant to stay in Egypt. "A little while, or six years," answered Bonaparte; "everything depends on circumstances. I shall colonize the country; bring over artists, all sorts of workmen, women, and actors. We are only twenty-nine; we shall be thirty-five: that's not old; these six years will see me, if all goes well, in India. Tell every one who speaks of our departure, that you are going to Brest. Say the same thing to your family."

Bonaparte was eager for action. He missed the smell of powder. All the time he was in Paris, between the Italian campaign and the Egyptian expedition, he continually wore his spurs, although he did not wear his uniform. Night and day, he kept a horse in his stable, saddled and bridled.

One moment, the Egyptian plan was nearly abandoned, because war with Austria seemed imminent; but the complications soon vanished, and the preparations were resumed with vigor. There were many who regretted Bonaparte's departure, and said that his real place was in France. "The Directory wishes to get you away," the poet Arnault told him; "France wishes to keep you. The Parisians blame your resignation; they are crying out more bitterly than ever against the government. Aren't you afraid they will at last cry out after you?" "The Parisians

cry, but they will never do anything; they are dis-
contented, but they are not unhappy. If I got on
horseback, no one would follow me; the time hasn't
come. We shall leave to-morrow."

# XXI.

## THE FAREWELL AT TOULON.

MAY 3, 1798, Bonaparte and Josephine, after dining quietly with Barras at the Luxembourg, went to the Théâtre Français, where Talma was acting in the *Macbeth* of Ducis. He was received as warmly as on the first days of his return. When the play was over, he went home, and started at midnight, taking with him, in his carriage, Eugene, Bourrienne, Duroc, and Lavalette. Paris knew nothing of his departure; and the next morning, when every one thought that he was in the rue de la Victoire, he was already well on his way to the South. With the desire of outwitting the English spies, who were still in ignorance of the destination of the expedition, he had made all his preparations quietly, and had not even let Josephine go to Saint Germain to bid farewell to her daughter, before leaving. Yet Josephine still did not know how long she would be away, and Bonaparte had not told her whether he should allow her to accompany him on this mysterious expedition on which he was about to start.

In his Memoirs, Marmont records an incident that came near having serious results for the party. At nightfall they had reached Aix-en-Provence, on their hurried journey to Toulon. Being eager to push on, without stopping at Marseilles, where they would in all probability have been delayed, they took a more direct road, through Roquevaire, a highway, but one less frequently taken than the other: for some days the postillions had not been that way. Suddenly, as they were rapidly going down the slope of a hill, the carriage was stopped by a violent shock. Every one sprang up, and got out of the carriage to see what was the matter. They found that a large branch of a tree stretching across the road had stopped the carriage. Ten steps further, at the foot of the descent, a bridge crossing a torrent over which they had to go had fallen down the previous evening. No one knew anything about it; and the carriage would have gone over the precipice, had not this branch stopped them at the edge. "Does not this seem like the hand of Providence?" asks Marmont. "Is not Bonaparte justified in thinking that it watches over him? Had it not been for this branch, so strangely placed, and strong enough to hold, what would have become of the conqueror of Egypt, the conqueror of Europe, whose power for fifteen years prevailed over the surface of the earth?"

On what trifles human destinies depend! In the eyes of Providence, men are but pygmies. If that branch had been a trifle thinner, it would have been all over with Napoleon: no battle of the Pyramids, no 18th Brumaire, no Consulate, no Empire, no coronation, no Austerlitz, no Waterloo! Were the ancients right when they said that those whom the gods love die young? And would it have been well for Napoleon to die at twenty-nine, before his greatest glories, but also before his misfortunes? Do not the men who are called indispensable live too long for themselves and for their country? Short as is human life, it is too long for them.

But in 1798 Bonaparte was far from making such reflections. When he reached Toulon, May 9, he was all pride, enthusiasm, hope. In Paris, he was smothering; at Toulon, he drew a full breath. In Paris, in the neighborhood of the Directors, he feared to seem to be their subordinate; and in his relations with them he assumed alternately an air of dignity and one of familiarity; but, as Madame de Staël said, "he failed in both. He is a man who is natural only when in command." At Toulon, he felt himself the master. He meant, to quote Madame de Staël again, "to become a poetic person, instead of remaining exposed to the gossip of Jacobins, which in this popular form is no less ingenious than that of courts." For all its animation and brilliancy, Paris had seemed a tomb, and he was glad to have lifted its heavy lid. In the presence of his army he felt himself a new man. The cheers of the soldiers and sailors, the clash of arms, the murmur of the waves, the voice of the trumpets, the roar of the drums, inspired him. He saw only the brilliant side of war. No one knew whither he was going: to what coast his fleet was bound — whether to Portugal or to England; to the Crimea or to Egypt. Did he mean to conquer the land of the Pharaohs? To pierce the Isthmus of Suez? To capture Jerusalem like Godfrey of Bouillon, and to penetrate into India, like Alexander? Those mysteries fired the imagination of the masses. The great interest in the expedition was due to ignorance of its destination. The same uncertainty prevailed over Europe, Africa, and Asia. England was anxiously wondering where the thunderbolt would fall.

The more perilous the adventure, the greater its charm for Bonaparte. He was like those riders who care only for a restive horse. It was a keen joy to him to stake everything and defy fortune. Throughout his career we find this love of the extraordinary, of the unknown, this desire to cope with obstacles generally thought insuperable. He always pursued victory as a hunter pursues his prey, as the gambler tries to win,—with a devouring passion. When he was about to leave his wife and country, any feeling of regret would have seemed to him unworthy of a man; a tear he would have thought a weakness. What he really loved, was no longer Josephine, but glory.

A few months before, he would perhaps have taken his wife with him to the wars; but now the lover has given place to the hero. He was to write to her no more love-letters such as he wrote from Italy. It was no longer Jean Jacques Rousseau who interested him; but Plutarch, the Bible, the Koran. As soon as they reached Toulon, he told Josephine that he could not take her to Egypt, since he was unwilling to expose her to the fatigues and dangers of the voyage, the climate, and the expedition. Josephine said that all these things had no terrors for a woman like her; that in three voyages she had already sailed more than five thousand leagues; that she was a creole and the heat of the East could do her no harm. Bonaparte, to console her, promised that she should follow within two months, when he should be settled in Egypt; and that he would send to fetch her the frigate *Pomone*, which had brought her to France the first time. So Josephine wrote to her daughter, May 15: "My dear Hortense, I have been for five days at Toulon; I was not tired by the journey, but was very sorry to have left you so suddenly without being able to say good by to you and to my dear Caroline. But I am somewhat consoled by the hope of seeing you again very soon. Bonaparte does not wish me to sail with him, but wants me to go to some watering-place before undertaking the voyage to Italy. He will send for me in two months. So, dear Hortense, I shall soon have the pleasure of pressing you to my heart, and of telling you how much I love you. Good by, my dear girl."

Bonaparte knew from the movements of the English that he had better be off without delay, but contrary winds kept him detained for ten days at Toulon.

He spent this time in addressing the army, completing the loading, and organizing a system of tactics. Five hundred sail were about to set forth on the Mediterranean. The fleet, which was supplied with water for a month, and with food for two months, carried about forty thousand men of all sorts, and ten thousand sailors. Five hundred grenadiers, accustomed to artillery, were placed on each three-decker, with orders, in case the English fleet was sighted, to bear down on it, and range alongside in order. Never had so vast a naval expedition been seen. Soldiers and sailors were full of confidence. Yet cooler heads, not carried away by warlike ardor and by the twofold fervor of youth and courage, were well aware of the great dangers which rendered the success of the expedition improbable, if not impossible.

Arnault, who sailed with the army, said that if the fleet had met the enemy on the voyage, it would have been lost, not because the flower of the Army of Italy was not present in sufficiently large numbers, but for the very opposite reason. Since they were distributed about in ships with their full quota of men already on board, the soldiers tripled on each ship the number of men necessary for its defence; and in such case everything superfluous is a positive disadvantage. If a fight had taken place, their movements would have been confused, the handling of the ships encumbered, and cannon-balls of the enemy would necessarily have found three men where, in ordinary circumstances, it would have found one or no one at all. Arnault also mentions the inconvenience produced by the artillery and its material: the shrouds were obstructed, the decks littered by it. "In case of attack, all would have had to be thrown into the sea, and we should have begun by sacrificing to defence the means of conquest. Even a victory would have ruined the expedition. We prayed Heaven that the generalissimo would not find himself compelled to win one!"

Marmont says the same thing, and that he would not undertake to justify an expedition made in the face of so many adverse chances. He adds that the ships were insufficiently equipped, the crew short-handed and ignorant, the men-of-war encumbered with troops and the artillery material which prevented proper handling; that this vast fleet, composed of sloops and vessels of every sort, would have been of necessity scattered, and even destroyed, by meeting any squadron; that it was impossible to count upon a victory, and even then a victory would not have saved the convoy. "For the expedition to succeed," Marmont goes on, "there was required a smooth voyage, and no sight of the enemy; but how expect such good luck in view of the enforced slowness of our progress, and of the pause we were to make before Malta? All the probabilities were then against us; we had not one chance in a hundred; we were sailing with a light heart to almost certain ruin. It must be acknowledged that we were playing a costly game, which even success would scarcely warrant."

Yet Bonaparte could not admit that Fortune would

be unkind to him. He had won so many favors from her that he deemed her his slave. He feared storms no more than he feared Nelson's ships. In his eyes obstacles were idle dreams. Returning, as well as going, he never thought of fearing the English cruisers. He said to himself, What can there be to fear for the ship that carries me and my fortune? But he was not alone in this faith in his destiny; he succeeded in communicating it to his companions. He believed in himself, and they believed in him. He had, in fact, reached one of those moments when great men sincerely imagine themselves above human nature, and look upon themselves as demi-gods.

May 19, the day of the departure, Nelson, the English admiral, was guarding the port. A violent squall, which damaged only one of the French frigates, drove the English fleet into the offing, and damaged it so severely that Nelson was obliged to withdraw for repairs, and he could not resume his station before Toulon till June 1, twelve days after the French fleet had sailed. The farewell of Bonaparte and Josephine was most touching. "All who have known Madame Bonaparte," says Bourrienne, "know that there have been few women so amiable. Her husband loved her passionately. He had carried her with him to Toulon, to see her until the last moment; could he know when he parted from her when he should see her again, even whether he should ever see her?"

The hour of departure had come. Bonaparte's

proclamation had found the hearts of all his men. "Soldiers, you have fought on mountain, plains, in sieges; there remains war at sea for you. The Roman legions, whom you have sometimes imitated, but not yet equalled, fought Carthage both on this sea and on the plains of Zama. Victory never deserted them, because they were brave, patient to endure fatigue, disciplined and united. The Genius of Liberty, which, since its birth, has made France the arbiter of Europe, demands that she become that of the seas and of the remotest nations." The fleet awaited the signal; the cannon of the ships replied to those of the forts. A vast multitude covering the heights above the port gazed with patriotic emotion on the imposing spectacle, which was lit by a brilliant sun. Josephine was on a balcony of the Intendant's house, trying to make out her husband, who was already embarked, through a spyglass. What was to become of the French fleet? Would it be able to get supplies at Malta? Would the impregnable fortress open its doors? Would he get to Egypt? Would they be able to land? Would they have to fight, not merely against the Mamelukes, but also against the numberless hordes of Turkey? What did it matter? Bonaparte believed himself master of fortune. Josephine was at once alarmed and proud, — alarmed at seeing her husband brave the equally fickle waves of the sea and of destiny; and proud of the cheers that saluted the departing hero. At a signal from the admiral's flagship, the sails were bent, the ships started, with a strong breeze from the north-west. But it was not without difficulty that the fleet got out of the roadstead. Many ships drag their anchors and are helpless. The *Orient*, carrying one hundred and twenty guns, on board of which was Bonaparte, careened so much as to cause great anxieties among the spectators upon the shore. Josephine trembled, but soon she was reassured; the vessel righted, and while the cheers of the multitude mingled with the music of the departing bands and the roar of the guns from the fleet and the forts, it sailed forth majestically upon the open sea.

## XXII.

JUST as in the most irascible natures a calm always follows violent wrath, so a city, however fiery its passions, cannot always remain in a paroxysm of energy or hate. After terrible popular crises there comes a lassitude which often ends in indifference or scepticism. A revolutionary song, the *Marseillaise*, for instance, at one moment arouses every one, and sounds like a sublime hymn ; at another, like an old-fashioned, worn-out chorus. Orators who a few months ago moved the masses suddenly resemble old actors who cannot draw. Of all cities in the world, Paris is perhaps the ficklest in its tastes and passions. During the Year VII. Paris was weary of everything except pleasures and military glory. Politics, literature, newspapers, parliamentary debates, had but little interest for a populace which for nearly ten years had seen such varied sights and endured such intense emotions.

As Théophile Lavallée has said : " Every one laughed at the Republic, not merely at its festivals and absurd dresses, but at its wisest institutions, at its purest men." A goddess of Reason would not have been able to walk through the streets without exciting the jests of the crowd. Patriotic processions began to be looked upon as masquerades. The club orators were regarded as tedious preachers. The vast majority of Parisians cared no more for the Jacobins than for the émigrés, and listened no more to the denunciations of the one party than to the lamentations of the other. There was no room for the Republican legend or for the Royalist. What ruled Paris was not an idea, but selfishness, the love of material joys, scornful indifference for every form of rule except that of the sword. Only a few sincere, honest Republicans, like the upright Gohier, remained true to their principles and determined strenuously to resist every attempt to found a dictatorship; but abandoned by public opinion, which, after having had liberty for its ideal, had got a new idol, and bowed down before force, these men, whose austerity no longer suited the manners of the day, found themselves estranged from all about them.

The Directory, too much tinctured by Royalism to suit the Republicans, too Republican for the Royalists, was no longer taken seriously. It inspired, not wrath, but contempt. The flatterers of Barras paid court to him merely with their lips; and he — for he was very clear-sighted — felt that he had come to the end of his tether. The following lines upon this democratic gentleman were passed from hand to hand: —

> " More than Nero is my viscount a despot;
> Strutting beneath his red cap
> This king of straw harangues in a tone
> At which the idler laughs low in his grime;
> 'Tis Harlequin, Pantaloon, or Jack pudding,
> Putting on the airs of Agamemnon."

The festivities of the Luxembourg had lost all their importance, and every one was watching the horizon where the rising sun should appear.

Paris was not conspicuous for morality. The resuscitation of the religious feeling, of which the publication of the *Génie du Christianisme* was to be the signal, was yet almost invisible. The worship of the Theophilanthropists, founded by La Réveillère Lepaux, one of the Directors, was a mere burlesque. The new religion imposed upon its adherents a very short creed. As the Goncourts have said: " It was a belief of the compactest form. Its temples were distinguished by the inscription: ' Silence and Respect; here God is worshipped.' It recommended virtue by means of handbills. With compilations from Greek and Chinese moralists, Theophilanthropy had pilfered the wisdom of nations to make of it a moral code. It rested on a library instead of on a tabernacle. Its *Pater Noster*, as proposed by one of the members of the sect, had expunged the phrase, *who art in heaven*, because God is omnipresent; also the phrase, *forgive us our trespasses as we forgive those who have trespassed against us*, because that is equivalent to saying imitate us; and finally the phrase, *lead us not into temptation*, on the ground that it changes God into a devil. Every one — Catholics, Jews, Protestants, Mohammedans — could be Theophilanthropists, preserving whatever they wanted of their religion. The feast days of the new worship were those of the Foundation of the Republic, of the Sovereignty of the People, of Youth, of Married People, of Agriculture, of Liberty, of Old Age. The priests of Theophilanthropy, by means of their prayers for all the acts of the government, secured official favor. The Catholic churches were allotted to them in common with their original possessors, and the same churches were open from six till eleven in the morning for the rites of Catholicism, and after eleven for those of the Theophilanthropists. But the sect of the hunchbacked Director — Mahomet, the Theophilanthropist, La Réveillère-laid-peau, as he was called — was to last but four years at the most, and to succumb to ridicule. This grotesque imitation of Christianity could no longer please the impious more than the devout, and wags were going to call this Æsop in office the pope of the *citoyens filoux-en-troupe* [gang of sharpers]."

Certainly it was not from this new sect that a reform in morals could come; other springs were demanded for the purification of society. Scandal became the order of the day. From the dregs of society there rose a swarm of upstarts, the product of speculation and immorality, who made a display of their cynical habits, their tasteless luxury, their grotesque conceit. The Republic possessed number-

less Turcarets. These upstarts tried to outdo the old
farmers-general. Royalists and Republicans vied in
viciousness and frivolity. Women's fashions became
abominably indecent. The parody of antiquity knew
no bounds. "By the restoration of Olympus," the
Goncourts have said, "the *Impossibles* of the new
France derived so much benefit that they tried gradually to introduce nakedness. The robe fell lower
upon the bosom, and arms which had been covered
to the elbow, being suspected of being ugly arms,
were bared to the shoulder. It was with the legs
and feet as it was with the arms. Jewelled thongs
were fastened about the ankles, —

> " ' The diamond alone should set off
> The charms which wool dishonors,' —

and gold rings were worn on the toes." For some
time even the chemise was abandoned as old-fashioned. " The chemise," it was said, " mars the figure,
and makes awkward folds; a well-made *juste* lost its
grace and precision by means of the waving and
awkward folds of this old garment. . . . Women
have worn chemises for nearly two thousand years;
it was an absurdly old fashion."

Nothing was more fatal to the health than those
fashions which required the sun of Greece, and were
yet worn by our French Aspasias through the fogs
and frost of our winters. Dr. Delessarts said,
towards the end of 1798, that he had seen more
young girls die since the fashion of gauze dresses

came in, than in the forty years before. The extravagant fashions were destined to last no longer than the sect of Theophilanthropists. The poet Panard represented Venus, at the last council of Olympus, as opposing these too transparent draperies: —

> " The charms that everywhere
> Without veil are admired to-day,
> By dint of speaking to the eye,
> Leave nothing to say to the heart."

Women have put on their chemises again, and decency resumed its rights.

Society gradually reorganized itself, but slowly and with difficulty. A few aristocratic drawing-rooms opened, but only to ridicule the new institutions, to sneer at men and things. The official world, in which appeared a few ambitious gentlemen, was crowded with intriguers, speculators, parasites, the flatterers of every form of power. If the drawing-rooms were rare, theatres, subscription balls, public gardens, cafés, tea-gardens, abounded. The Café Véry, the balls of Richelieu, of Tivoli, of Marbeuf, the Pavilion of Hanover, Frascati, were fashionable, and the motley throng that filled them did not prevent good society crowding them for amusement. The families of the victims did not mind meeting the executioners. Why hate one another, after all? Who knows, the foes of yesterday may be the allies of the morrow! Royalists and Jacobins had a common enemy, the Directory, which had perse-

cuted each in turn.   Conquerors and conquered, pro-
scribers and proscribed, met in the same dance.

People of the old régime plunged into amusement
like the rest, with hearty zeal, but yet with some
alarm.   Who could pass through the Place de la
Révolution without recalling the scaffold?   Blood-
stains still seemed to mark the stones.   And the
18th Fructidor, the transportation to Cayenne, the
dry guillotine, as it was called, made the blood run
cold.   However short a Parisian's memory, those
events were of too recent a date for him not to dread
the future.   The survivors of the Jacobins had
opened the Club du Manège.   It had not the renown
of the old clubs, but it was still alarming, and the
orators' voices sounded like a funeral knell.   The
enemies of liberty and friends of the approaching
dictatorship never forgot to recall the red spectre
against the Republic.   Without suspecting it, all
parties were preparing to play Bonaparte's game.
This man, who bewitched France, was to persuade
all, without saying a word, that he was the protector
and saviour of every one.   Everything was to
crumble into ruins; only one man would be left.   Of
the Republican legend, only the military side sur-
vived.   Those who were tired of speeches were eager
for bulletins of victories.   The Parisian public
became more interested in the shores of the Nile
than in those of the Seine.   News from Bonaparte
became more interesting, as English cruisers made
it even more difficult and rarer.   As Madame

de Staël said, "letters dated Cairo, orders issued from Alexandria to go to the ruins of Thebes, near the boundaries of Ethiopia, augmented the reputation of a man who was not seen, but who appeared from afar like an extraordinary phenomenon. . . . Bonaparte skilfully utilizing the enthusiasm of the French for military glory, allied their pride with his victories as with his defeats. Gradually he acquired with all people the place the Revolution had held, and gathered about his name all the national feeling which had made France great before the world."

The period of incubation of the dictatorship is a most interesting study. Paris of the Year VII. explains Paris of the Consulate and of the Empire. The change was made in morals and manners before it appeared in politics. There is something strange in the fluctuation of the Parisian between liberty that is license and order which is despotism. This illogical and fickle populace is in turn the most ungovernable and the most docile in the world. Everything lies in knowing whether it is in a period of agitation or of repose. When it is agitated, it would break any sword, any sceptre. When it is at peace, it asks its masters only to guard its slumbers.

## XXIII.

WE have just glanced at Paris in the Year VII. Let us now see what place was taken there by Madame Bonaparte, her relatives and friends, and the society of which she formed a part.

Josephine did not return directly to Paris after her husband sailed from Toulon, but went to Plombières for the waters, and stayed there three months. She met with an alarming accident there : a wooden balcony on which she was standing with several ladies of her acquaintance, gave way, and she was severely bruised by the fall, so that for some days she was in danger. At Plombières she received her first tidings from the Egyptian expedition, from the capture of Malta to that of Cairo, and learned from Bonaparte's letters that she must give up all hope of joining him there. Later she heard that the *Pomone*, the ship in which she meant to sail to Egypt, had returned to France, and had been captured by an English cruiser just as it had left the harbor of Toulon.

At the end of September, 1798, Josephine returned to Paris and bought the estate of Malmaison, near the village of Rueil. It cost one hundred and sixty thousand francs, and she paid for it in part with her dowry, in part with her husband's money. Here she passed the late autumn of 1798 and the summer of 1799. The winter she spent in Paris in her little house in the rue de la Victoire.

Her position at this time was not a wholly happy one. No one knew when her husband would come back from Egypt. He had himself told her when he left that he might be gone five or six years; and possibly he carried with him some suspicions about his wife which had been carefully strengthened by Joseph and Lucien, who were jealous of their sister-in-law's influence over their brother. Josephine's detractors asserted that she was untrue to her husband, but they could give no proof of their insinuations. Besides, when there is no public scandal, history has no right to pry into such matters. For all their malevolence, Bonaparte's brothers were unable to tarnish the reputation of a woman who, far from her husband and son, had no one to defend her.

Madame de Rémusat describes, in her Memoirs, a visit which she and her mother, Madame de Vergennes, made at Malmaison. "Madame Bonaparte," she says, "was naturally expansive, and even somewhat indiscreet; and she had no sooner seen my mother than she confided to her a number of things about her absent husband, her brothers-in-law, in short, about a world of which we knew nothing. Bonaparte was looked upon as lost to France; his wife was neglected. My mother took pity on her; we paid her some attentions, which she never forgot." Does not this language betray some of the scorn which the people of the old régime felt for the new ?

Legitimist society had no more respect for Bonaparte than for the other prominent persons of the Revolution, and tried to turn to ridicule this family of insignificant Corsican gentry who would have cut such a modest figure at the court of Louis XIV. It found fault with Madame Bonaparte for her relations with Madame Tallien and the set of the Directory. The habitués of Coblentz did not respect even military glory, and those who, a few years later, were to throng the Emperor's palace, spoke contemptuously of the Republican general. If the hero of Arcole had fanatical admirers, he had also implacable detractors. When he was leaving for Egypt, these satirical lines were in circulation : —

> " What talents are thrown into the water !
> What fortunes squandered !
> How many are hastening to the grave,
> To carry Bonaparte to the clouds !
> This warrior is worth his weight in gold.
> In France no one doubts this ;
> But he would be worth still more
> If he were worth what he costs us."

Madame Bonaparte, whose main interest lay in the fragments of the Faubourg Saint Germain, suffered much from these pin-pricks. She especially dreaded the beautiful and caustic Madame de Contades, daughter and sister of the MM. de Bouillé, whose name is inseparably connected with the affair of Varennes. "Everything about her was eccentric," says the Duchess of Abrantès, speaking of this lady, who had recently returned to France. "She was not melancholy, — far from it, — yet no one would have dared to laugh in the room where she was, unless she had set the example. Her hatred for Bonaparte was most amusing. She would not even acknowledge that he deserved his reputation. 'Come, come,' she used to say when my mother spoke of all his victories in Italy and Egypt; 'I could do as much with a glance.'"

Let us listen to the Duchess of Abrantès as she describes a ball at the Thélusson mansion (at the end of the rue Cerutti, now rue Laffitte). "'Who are those two ladies?' asked Madame de Damas of the old Marquis d'Hautefort, on whose arm she was. 'What! don't you recognize the Viscountess de Beauharnais? That is she with her daughter. She is now Madame Bonaparte. Stop! Here is a place at her side; sit down here, and renew your acquaintance.' Madame de Damas's sole reply was to shove the old marquis so hard that she hustled him into one of the little rooms before the large rotunda. 'Are you mad?' she asked when they were in the other room. 'A nice place, upon my word, next to Madame Bonaparte! Ernestine would have had to be introduced to her daughter. You are beside yourself, Marquis.' 'Not at all! Why in the world shouldn't Ernestine make her acquaintance, or even become a friend of Mademoiselle Hortense de Beauharnais? She is a charming person, gentle and amiable.' 'What difference does that make to me? I don't want to have anything to do with such women. I don't like people who dishonor their misfortunes.' The Marquis d'Hautefort shrugged his shoulders and made no reply."

Many Royalists could not forgive Bonaparte either the 13th Vendémiaire or his indirect participation in the 18th Fructidor, and blamed Josephine for her friendship with regicides. They thought that these ties on the part of the wife of a guillotined nobleman ill became her birth and antecedents, and that in her new position there was something like apostasy. She consoled herself, however, for the intensity of some of the Legitimists with others who, with more forethought, were already paying their court to her in anticipation of the near future. The Marquis of Caulaincourt (the father of the future Duke of Vicenza) saw her very often and gave her wise advice. In the drawing-room of Madame de Permon (mother of the future Duchess of Abrantès) she met all that was left of the former society of the Faubourg Saint Germain, and the brilliant circle of fashionable young men, — de Noailles, de Montcalm, de Perigord, de Montron, de Rastignac, de l'Aigle, de Montaigu, de la Feuillade, de Sainte-Aulaire. Josephine appeared very well in this centre of elegance. The life of Paris suited her to a charm. She liked balls, dinner-par-

ties, concerts, the theatre, pleasure-parties. She was
a delightful hostess, and presided with great success
over a circle of friends and admirers. Her Thursday
receptions in the rue de la Victoire were deservedly
famous. Among the women she knew intimately
were the Countess Fanny de Beauharnais, Madame
Caffarelli, the Countess of Houdetot, Madame Andréossy, and the two rival beauties, Madame Tallien
and Madame Regnault de Saint-Jean-d'Angély. Although indifferently educated, Josephine had a vague
notion of literature, and gladly received famous writers and artists. It was at her house, at the time of
the Egyptian expedition, that Legouvé read his *Mérite
des Femmes*, and that Bailly recited his drama, the
*Abbé de l'Epée*. In her drawing-room there used to
meet Bernardin de Saint-Pierre, Ducis, Lemercier,
Joseph Chénier, Méhul, Talma, Volney, Andrieux,
Picard, Colin d'Harleville, Baour-Lormian, Alexan-
dre Duval.

With the Bonapartes Josephine exercised diplo-
macy. With great tact she concealed her discontent
with them, and avoided an open breach with any of
the members of this vindictive family, who were all
annoyed by her influence over Napoleon. Before he
left for Egypt he had desired to see his mother and
brothers and sisters comfortably settled in Paris. Although younger than Joseph, he already regarded
himself as the head of the Bonaparte family, and was
determined to assert his authority. In his absence,
his mother, Madame Letitia, who was born at Leg-

horn in 1750, and still preserved traces of marvellous beauty, still held much control over her children. She was a woman of great energy, with an impetuous character and an iron will, firm to the point of obstinacy, economical even to avarice for herself, but generous to the poor, and lavish so far as her son Napoleon's glory was concerned; she was kind at heart, though with a cold exterior, but with no breeding. Madame Letitia, who was rather a Roman matron than a modern woman, never forgave Josephine her frivolous ways, her extravagance, her inordinate love of dress. She would have preferred for Napoleon a more serious and more economical wife, and deeply regretted a marriage which she thought had not made her son happy.

Joseph, the oldest child, was an honest man, gentle, sympathetic, well-bred, straightforward; his manners were courteous, his face was attractive. He was born in 1768, and had married, at the end of 1794, a rich young woman of Marseilles, Mademoiselle Marie Julie Clary, and was the possessor of a moderate fortune for that time. After being Ambassador of the French Republic at Rome, he had returned to Paris, bringing with him his wife's sister, Mademoiselle Désirée Clary, whom Napoleon had wished to marry. At that time she was in deep affliction on account of the tragic death of General Duphot, who had been killed at Rome, almost before her eyes, shortly before the day set for their marriage. After a few months of mourning, she was consoled, and August 16, 1798, while living with her brother-in-law, Joseph, in the rue du Rocher, she married the future King of Sweden, Bernadotte.

Lucien, who was born in 1775, was the youngest of the Deputies of the Council of Five Hundred. He possessed a rare intelligence, was well educated, and had a real passion for letters. He wrote much, composed verses, and aspired for fame of all sorts. He was a ready speaker, familiar with antiquity, a man of both imagination and action, and skilfully furthered his brother's glory and interests. He was active, ardent, full of resources, and, in spite of his youth, he exercised considerable influence on his colleagues in the Council of Five Hundred. He was considered a Republican, and he was one in fact; and even on the 18th Brumaire he imagined that he was still loyal to the Revolutionary cause. In 1794 he had held a modest position as warehouseman in a little province village of the name of Saint Maximin, which, after 1793, had assumed the name of Marathon. He adopted the name of Brutus. Citizen Brutus Bonaparte — for so the future Prince of Canino was called — fell in love with a pretty and respectable girl, Christine Boyer, whose father was an innkeeper at Saint Maximin. Lucien married her, and Napoleon was furious at a marriage which he looked upon as most unsuitable; but Madame Lucien Bonaparte, who was handsome and gentle, soon acquired the manners of good society, and was perfectly at home in the finest drawing-room.

Louis Bonaparte, who was born in 1779, had accompanied Napoleon to Egypt, but returned to Paris with despatches. Although later he was to prove more hostile to Josephine than either Joseph or Lucien, before the 18th Brumaire he maintained friendly relations with his sister-in-law, who perhaps thought of him as a son-in-law.

The youngest of Napoleon's brothers, Jerome, was born in 1784; he was lively, amiable, intelligent, clever; but rattle-pated, turbulent, fond of pleasure, and tired of always having Eugene de Beauharnais spoken of as the model whom he should imitate.

Madame Letitia lived in the rue du Rocher with her son Joseph and his wife, an agreeable and worthy woman. Of Napoleon's three sisters, the eldest, Elisa, who was born in 1777, and married in 1797 to Felix Bacciochi, lived in the grande rue Verte, like Lucien. The second, Pauline, who was born in 1780, and during the Italian campaign had married General Leclerc, lived in the rue de la Ville l'Évêque. Caroline, who was born in 1782, was finishing her education at Madame Campan's school at Saint Germain, where she was a companion of Hortense de Beauharnais.

All these girls had inherited their mother's beauty, especially Pauline, who was called the handsomest woman in Paris, and was the belle of every ball at which she was present. With the ambition of a daughter of Cæsars, and her irresistible beauty, she triumphed in every drawing-room as did her brother on the battle-field. She was one of those coquettes who wring from the public a cry of admiration and surprise as soon as they appear in sight; who make the most of all their advantages, and, regarding the world as a stage, are, so to speak, artistic beauties. Madame Leclerc was moderately fond of her sister-in-law, Josephine, who, although older and less beautiful, held a much more important position in the Paris world. As for Caroline Bonaparte, she promised not only to possess great beauty, but even a more ambitious spirit than her sister Pauline.

It was not easy for Josephine to remain even on decorous, not to say affectionate, terms with this large and powerful family. Already the antagonism between the Bonapartes and the Beauharnais began to manifest itself; and the intrigues, the jealousies, the contesting influences to be seen in courts, appeared under the Republic, even before Napoleon attained power. The house in the rue de la Victoire was, so to speak, a palace of the Tuileries on a small scale; in it could be discerned the rising germs of the ambitions, heart-burnings, quarrels, which were to flourish full-grown under the Consulate and the Empire.

Besides these family annoyances, Josephine was often short of money. She spent vast sums on dress, and displayed that combination of luxury and want which distinguishes thriftless people. She owned costly jewels, and often lacked money to pay the most insignificant debts. Madame de Rémusat tells us that at this period Madame Bonaparte showed her, at Malmaison, " the prodigious quantity of pearls, diamonds, and cameos which she possessed; they were already worthy to figure in the *Thousand and One Nights*, and were yet to be added to enormously. Italy, grateful after the invasion, had contributed to this abundance, and particularly the Pope, who was touched by the consideration displayed by the conqueror in denying himself the pleasure of planting his banners on the walls of Rome." Madame de Rémusat adds that the owner of these treasures, whose place was filled with pictures, statues, and mosaics, was often in want.

But Josephine bore her troubles very lightly; and the money troubles that beset her did not distress her beyond measure, for she had no doubts of the happy fortune that awaited her. Amiable, affectionate, insinuating, with gentle manners, an even temper, a deep voice, a kindly face, Josephine was a charming woman. Never offending any one, never disposed to argue about politics or anything else, distinctly obliging, endowed with that careless grace that distinguishes creoles, anxious to win every one's sympathy, pleasing people of every social position, she also possessed most fully the rare quality which covers every fault and is especially attractive in women, — kindliness. Royalists forgave the Republican origin of the hero of the 13th Vendémiaire, when they said, " His wife is so kind." People who had dreaded a presentation to Bonaparte paid homage to Josephine. We shall see, under the Consulate, peo-

ple of the old régime visiting Madame Bonaparte on
the ground floor, without going a story higher, where
the First Consul lived. Josephine, while seeking
Legitimist society, took care to be well received in
Republican society. She went to all the entertainments of the Directory, and secured the good graces
of the official world. Her relations with Barras,
who had been one of the witnesses at her wedding,
and the main author of her good fortune, continued
to be excellent. She especially cultivated the friendship of a Republican lady of austere virtue, — Madame
Gohier, wife of one of the Directors. She thought,
and rightly, that intimacy with a woman whose reputation was spotless would defend her own. Moreover,
the Gohier conciliated those Republicans whose instinctive dread of her husband's ambition needed to
be allayed.

According to Josephine, Bonaparte was the purest
of patriots, and those who dared to doubt this were
moved by malice or envy. This woman, in spite of her
frivolous, insignificant appearance, intrigued like an
experienced diplomatist. She did not think herself
skilful, yet she was; just as many think they are,
and are not. The greatest men have been aided by
women, whether they knew it or not. Without Josephine, it is probable that Napoleon would never
have become Emperor. It was in vain that he told
her not to talk politics or to meddle with affairs: she
was still the most efficient aid to his plans, and during his absence she prepared the field on which he
was to show himself the master.

## XXIV.

TACITUS uttered a profound truth when he said, "*Major e longinquo reverentia*," which may be thus translated: "Distance adds to glory." Bonaparte in Egypt became for the Parisians an epic hero; the Pyramids were the pedestal of his glory. The forty centuries of their history became the prologue of his career. Egypt, Palestine, Syria, those famous and wonderful names, what memories they called forth: the Pharaohs, the Holy Land, Christ, the Crusaders, the Bible, the Gospel, the Delivery of Jerusalem! Bonaparte, who wrapt himself in his fame, like Talma in a Roman toga; Bonaparte, who said, "It's imagination that rules the world"; Bonaparte, who during all the acts of the great drama of his life, kept thinking of the Parisians as Alexander ever thought of the Athenians, had conjectured the effect which such an expedition would produce on the democratic chivalry, sprung from the Revolution, and felt the same ardor, the same courage, the same thirst for adventures as the old French nobility. Did the Crusaders display more audacity or heroism than the companions of the conqueror of the Pyramids, and is there a Golden Book greater than the collection of his proclamations, in which are inscribed the imperishable names of so many brave men?

Heated by the sun, fired by perpetual victory, the young general conceived gigantic plans. Nowhere did this poet who carried out in life his visions feel so fully at ease as in this old land of Egypt, which opened its vast and brilliant horizons before him. Even after his coronation, after Austerlitz, he was to regret this land of his dreams, where he had planned the conquest of Africa, and Asia, and then of Europe, attacked from behind. Plutarch was not enough for this soul tormented by a colossal ambition. His books were the Bible and the Koran. His Titanic imagination filled with Hebrew and Mahometan poetry, strayed in unknown and infinite regions. Later he told Madame de Rémusat what he felt at this strange period of his life, when nothing seemed impossible. "In Egypt," he said, "I found myself free from the bonds of a hindering civilization; I dreamed strange dreams and saw the way to put them into action; I created a religion; I fancied myself on the way to Asia on an elephant's back, a turban on my head, and in my hand a new Alcoran, composed by me. In my enterprises I should have concentrated the experiences of two worlds, exploring for my own use the region of all histories, attacking the English power in India, and thereby renewing my relations with the old Europe."

What a succession of amazing pictures! what varied scenes! what picturesque visions! The Nile, the Pyramids, the Mamelukes, their terrible cavalry dashing itself to pieces against the squares; the triumphal entrance into Cairo; the Arabs in the mosque singing, "Let us sing the loving-kindness of the great Allah! Who is he who has saved from the perils of the sea and the wrath of his enemies the son of Victory? Who is he who has led to the shores of the Nile the brave men of the West? It is the great Allah, who is no longer wroth with us!" Listen to the Oriental dialogue between Bonaparte and the Mufti in the Pyramid: —

"*Bonaparte.* Glory be to Allah! There is no God but God, and Mahomet is his prophet. The bread stolen by the wicked man turns to dust in his mouth.

" *The Mufti.* Thou hast spoken like the wisest of Mollahs.

"*Bonaparte.* I can bring down from heaven a chariot of fire and drive it on earth.

" *The Mufti.* Thou art the greatest captain, and art armed with power."

Bonaparte's condition in Egypt was at the same time one of grandeur and of distress. If at certain moments his ambition and pride fired him with the belief that he was not merely a conqueror but also a prophet, the founder of a religion, a demigod, at other times he was brought back to the reality by the cruel force of destiny. His soul was filled with mingled enthusiasm and melancholy, with a frantic passion for glory and an utter contempt for all earthly vanities. The melancholy from which he had already suffered in the Italian campaign attacked him again in Egypt, and perhaps more severely. It inspired this letter to his brother Joseph, written at Cairo, July 25th, 1798: "You will see in the public prints the result of the battles and the conquest of Egypt, which was hotly enough disputed to add a new leaf to the military glory of this army. . . . I have many domestic trials. . . . Your friendship is very dear to me; nothing is needed to make me a misanthrope except to lose you and see you betray me. It is a sad condition to have at once every sort of feeling for the same person in one heart. Arrange for me to have a country-place when I return, either near Paris or in Burgundy. I mean to pass the winter there in solitude; I am disgusted with human nature; greatness palls upon me; my feelings are all withered. Glory is trivial at twenty-nine; nothing is left me but to become a real egoist. I mean to keep my house; I shall never give it to any one whatsoever. I have not enough to live on. Farewell, my only friend; I have never been unjust to you."

In Egypt, as in Italy, Bonaparte's heart was torn with jealousy. He had doubts of Josephine's feelings, of her fidelity, and this thought pursued him even in his military occupations in Syria. Amid all these adventures and perils his imagination often turned to Paris. He forgot the East in thinking of the little house in the rue de la Victoire, and the fair image of Josephine appeared to him, always fascinating, but at times disturbing. He imagined her at the Luxembourg, at the entertainments of Barras, surrounded by young musicians and adorers whom perhaps she encouraged by her smiles. This is what is narrated by Bourrienne, who was present at an outburst of suspicious wrath before the fountains of Messudiah, near El-Arish.

Bonaparte was walking alone with Junot; his face, always pale, had become paler than usual. His features were uneasy, his eye wild. After talking with Junot for a quarter of an hour, he left him and went up to Bourrienne. "You are not devoted to me," he said roughly. "Women! Josephine!—If you were devoted to me, you would have told me what I have just learned from Junot. He is a true friend. Josephine—and I'm six hundred leagues away! You ought to have told me. Josephine!—to deceive me in that way! She!—Confound them! I will wipe out the whole brood of coxcombs and popinjays!—As for her! divorce!—yes, divorce! a public divorce! a full exposure!—I must write! I know everything. You ought to have told me."

Is not this like Shakspeare's *Othello?*

> "Look here, Iago;
> All my fond love thus do I blow to heaven: 'tis gone.--
> Arise, black vengeance, from thy hollow hell!
> Yield up, O love! thy crown, and hearted throne,
> To tyrannous hate! swell, bosom, with thy fraught,
> For 'tis of aspics' tongues!"

Bonaparte's face changed, his voice broke.

> "O! beware, my lord, of jealousy;
> It is the green-eyed monster, which doth mock
> The meat it feeds on : that cuckold lives in bliss,
> Who, certain of his fate, loves not his wronger:
> But, O! what damned minutes tells he o'er,
> Who dotes, yet doubts; suspects, yet strongly loves!"

Bourrienne tried to calm the general; he blamed Junot for a lack of generosity in thus lightly accusing a woman who was absent and unable to defend herself. "No," he went on; "Junot does not prove his devotion by adding domestic trials to the uneasiness you feel over the situation of his companions at the beginning of a hazardous enterprise." Bonaparte was not pacified; he kept muttering something about divorce. Bourrienne spoke to him about his glory. "My glory!" he replied; "I don't know what I wouldn't give to know that what Junot has told me is not true, so much do I love that woman! If Josephine is guilty, a divorce must separate us forever. . . . I don't wish to be the laughing-stock of all the idlers in Paris. I am going to write to my brother Joseph; he will see to the divorce."

Nevertheless, Bonaparte softened a little, and Bourrienne at once availed himself of the moment to say: "A letter may be intercepted; it will betray the anger that dictated it; as for the divorce, there is time enough for that later, when you shall have reflected." Bourrienne in this case was a wiser counsellor than Junot, and Bonaparte did well to listen to his secretary rather than to his fellow-soldier.

His jealousy was so wild at this time, that he discussed it with his step-son, Josephine's own child, Eugene de Beauharnais, who says in his Memoirs: " The commander-in-chief began to have great causes of annoyance, from the discontent which prevailed in a certain part of the army, especially among some generals, as well as from news he received from France, where attempts were made to undermine his domestic happiness. Though I was young, I inspired him with so much confidence that he spoke to me of his sufferings. It was generally in the evening that he made his complaints and confidence, striding up and down his tent. I was the only one to whom he could unbosom himself freely. I tried to soften his anger; I consoled him as well as I could, — so far as my youth and my respect for him permitted."

The situation of a youth of seventeen receiving confidences of that sort is, at the least, a delicate one. In the whole matter he showed tact and a precocious wisdom, for which Bonaparte was grateful. " The harmony existing between my step-father and me," he says, " was nearly broken by the following incident: General Bonaparte had been paying attentions to an officer's wife, and sometimes drove out with her in a barouche. She was a clever woman, and not bad-looking. At once the rumor ran that she was his mistress; so that my position as aide-de-camp and step-son of the General became very painful. Since it was part of my duty to accompany the General, who never went out without an aide-de-camp,

I had already had to follow this barouche; but I felt so humiliated that I called on General Berthier to ask for a place in his regiment. A somewhat lively interview between my step-father and me was the result of this step; but from that moment he discontinued his drives in a barouche with that lady, and he never treated me any less well on account of it."

Of the eight aides-de-camp whom Bonaparte took with him to Egypt, four perished there, — Julien, Sulkowski, Croisier, and Guibert; two were wounded, Duroc and Eugene de Beauharnais; Merlin and Lavalette alone got through safe and sound. If there was a dangerous duty, — to ride into the desert and reconnoitre the bands of Arabs or Mamelukes, — Eugene was always the first to volunteer. One day, when he was hastening forward with his usual eagerness, Bonaparte called him back, saying, "Young man, remember that in our business we must never seek danger; we must be satisfied with doing our duty, and doing it well, and leave the rest to God!"

Another time, during the siege of Saint Jean d'Acre, the commander-in-chief sent an officer with an order to the most exposed position; he was killed. Bonaparte sent another, who was also killed; and so with a third. The order had to go, and Bonaparte had only two aides with him — Eugene de Beauharnais and Lavalette. He beckoned to the latter to come forward, and said to him in a low voice, so that Eugene should not hear: "Lavalette, take this order. I don't want to send this boy, and have him killed so young; his mother has entrusted him to me. You know what life is. Go!"

Another day, also before Saint Jean d'Acre, a piece of shell struck Eugene de Beauharnais in the head: he fell, and lay for a long time under the ruins of a wall which the shell had knocked down. Bonaparte thought he was killed, and uttered a cry of grief. Eugene was only wounded, and at the end of nineteen days he asked leave to resume his post, in order to take part in the other assaults, which failed, like the first, in spite of Bonaparte's obstinacy. "This wretched hole," he said to Bourrienne, "has cost me a good deal of time and a great many men; but things have gone too far; I must try one last assault. If it succeeds, the treasury, the arms of Djezzar, whose fierceness all Syria curses, will enable me to arm three hundred thousand men. Damascus calls me; the Druses are waiting for me; I shall enlarge my army; I shall announce the abolition of the tyranny of the pashas, and shall reach Constantinople at the head of these masses. Then I shall overthrow the Turkish Empire, and found a new and great one; I shall make my place for posterity, and then perhaps I shall return to Paris by Vienna, destroying the house of Austria." All this was but a dream. It was in vain that Bonaparte's obstinacy lashed itself into a fury. It was to no purpose that he stood on a redoubt, with arms crossed, his eye fixed, a target for all the guns of the town, and commanded a final effort. His army, being destitute of artillery, had to raise the siege and return to Egypt. There was an end to the conquest of Asia Minor, the entrance into Constantinople, the attack on Europe in the rear, and a triumphal return to France by the banks of the Danube and Germany ! Bonaparte was not to be the Emperor of the East, and in speaking with vexation of the English commodore who defended Saint Jean d'Acre, he said: "That Sidney Smith made me miss my fortune." But how skilfully he managed to conceal his failure, and to paint the Syrian expedition with brilliant colors ! What cleverness in his proclamation of May 17, 1799: "Soldiers, you have crossed the desert that separates Africa from Asia more swiftly than an Arab army. The army which was marching to invade Egypt is destroyed ; you have captured its general, its wagons, its supply of water, its camels. You have taken possession of all the strong places that defended the oases. You have scattered in the fields of Mount Tabor the swarms of men who had gathered from all parts of Asia, in the hope of pillaging Egypt. . . . A few days more, and you hoped to take the Pasha himself in his palace ; but, at this season, the capture of the fortress of Acre is not worth the loss of a few days; the brave men whom I should have had to lose there are now required for more important operations."

In spite of great privations and of a heat of 107° F., the army took only twenty-five days, seventeen of which were spent in marching, to make the one hundred and nineteen leagues that separate Saint Jean

d'Acre from Cairo. Bonaparte re-entered this city
like an ancient general on the day of his triumph.
The procession resembled that of a conquering
Pharaoh, with its Oriental magnificence, its music,
and the applause. The captured enemy opened the
march; then came soldiers bearing the flags taken
from the Turks. The French garrison of Cairo and
the leading men of the city went as far as the suburb
of Coublé, to see the man whom the Arabs called
Sultan Kebir, the Sultan of Fire. The Sheik el
Bekri, a revered descendant of the Prophet, offered
him a magnificent horse, with a saddle adorned with
gold and pearls, and the young slave who held his
bridle. This slave was Rustan, the Mameluke of the
future Emperor. Other presents were also offered:
slaves, white and black, superb arms, costly rings,
dromedaries renowned for their speed, scent-boxes
filled with incense and perfumes. Preceded by the
Muftis and Ulemas of the mosque of Gama el Azhar,
the hero of Mount Tabor, with all the majesty of a
Sesostris, entered Cairo by the Gate of Victories, Bab
el Nasr.

A few days later the Turkish army, which had
assembled at Rhodes, appeared, escorted by Sidney
Smith's fleet, in sight of Alexandria, and anchored at
Aboukir. The Turks landed, to the number of eighteen thousand. Bonaparte marched out to meet them,
and, July 24, destroyed the entire army. That evening Kléber said, as he embraced him, "General, you
are as great as the world!" But the hour was draw-

ing nigh when the hero of Aboukir was about to
return to France. Fate had robbed him of his Oriental glory; his fortune was going to change the scene.
He was to be neither an Alexander nor a Mahomet,
but a Charlemagne. For six months he had received
no news from France. He sent a flag of truce to the
enemy's fleet to try to get some information under
pretext of arranging an exchange of prisoners. Sidney Smith took a malign pleasure in communicating
to Bonaparte a long list of disasters: the coalition
victorious; the natural boundaries of France abandoned; the Rhine recrossed; Italy lost; the fruits of
so many efforts and so many victories destroyed.
"Knowing General Bonaparte to be deprived of
news," said the English commodore, "I hope to be
agreeable to him in sending him a fresh batch of
papers." Bonaparte received them in the night of
August 3, and read them till morning with a mixture
of curiosity and wrath. At that moment his plan
was formed; he determined to return to France, in
spite of the vigilance of the English cruisers. A lack
of water and an accident to one of the ships compelled
the enemy to raise the blockade, and so favored his
departure. Meanwhile he kept his secret to himself,
went up the Nile to Cairo, stayed there six days, pretended to be summoned to an inspection in the province of Damietta, and returned mysteriously to the
neighborhood of Alexandria. He made Rear-Admiral
Gantheaume prepare two frigates, the *Muiron* and the
*Carrière*, and two despatch-boats, the *Revanche* and

the *Fortune.* It was between the arm of the Nile and Pharillon that he was to embark with a few companions, — Murat, Berthier, Eugene de Beauharnais, Bourrienne, and one or two others, — in the night of August 22. Sidney Smith did not even suspect so rash and unlikely a project.

Prince Eugene, in his Memoirs, thus describes this departure, which reads like a bit of romance: "As we drew near Alexandria, I was sent down to the edge of the sea to ascertain if our preparations for departure had been observed. On my return, the General interrogated me somewhat anxiously, but his face was soon lit with satisfaction when I told him that I had seen two frigates, but that they seemed to carry the French flag. In fact, he had every reason to be satisfied, since he saw his plan successful; for these two frigates were to carry us to France. He informed me of this at once, saying, 'Eugene, you are going to see your mother.' These words did not give me the joy I should have expected. We embarked that very night, and I noticed that my companions shared my awkwardness and sadness. The mystery surrounding our departure, regret at leaving our brave companions, the fear of being captured by the English, and our faint hope of ever seeing France, may explain this feeling."

Bonaparte alone had no doubts of a safe journey. A dead calm delayed the frigate in which he had just embarked. Gantheaume was discouraged, and proposed that he return to shore. "No," he answered

the admiral. "Don't be uneasy; we shall get off."
The next day, August 23, at sunrise, the calm continued, but at nine in the morning the wind rose, and
Bonaparte, bidding Egypt an eternal farewell, put
out to sea, sure that fortune would not betray him.

# XXV.

## THE RETURN FROM EGYPT.

THE Egyptian campaign was of little service to France, but to Napoleon it was most useful. It gave strange, mysterious quality to his glory, and placed him on an equality with the men who most impress the popular imagination; with Alexander, Cæsar, and Mahomet. Napoleon also had the gift of keeping his successes prominent, and letting his defeats sink out of sight. When he returned from Syria, after a serious check, he made the authorities of Cairo receive him with as much distinction as if he had taken Saint Jean d'Acre. He effaced the memory of the naval defeat of Aboukir by winning on land a victory called by the same name. Egypt is remote; the French at home noticed only the more brilliant points of the expedition, and all the failures sunk out of sight in a success which was thought to be decisive, though it was really only ephemeral.

Bonaparte staked everything on one throw by leaving his army. If he had been captured by the English cruisers, he would have been severely blamed by the public, and all their accusations would perhaps

NAPOLEON BONAPARTE

have crushed in the egg the imperial eagle, to use the poet's phrase. If great men would cease to be infatuated about themselves and would honestly analyze their glory, they would see that they often owe more to chance than to skill; that they won when they ought to have lost, and lost when they should have gained; and that the applause of the multitude accompanies success rather than merit. Of all Napoleon's conceptions, the campaign in France was doubtless the finest, but it was a failure. His Egyptian expedition, according to his greatest admirers, was badly planned, and yet it proved a stepping-stone to the throne. When men of strong character succeed, they explain their blunders which have turned out well by saying that they had confidence in their star, and never doubted the result. This fatalism has no real foundation. How many of these pretended stars vanish from the sky of politics! These men are in fact gamblers who excuse their love of adventure with the first pretext that occurs to them, to atone for their audacity and impress the popular spirit. For our part, we have little faith in this sort of fatalism, of which the inventors are the first victims.

The whole Egyptian campaign was made up of rashness and risks. It was only by a miracle that the invaders were able to arrive there without being scattered by the English fleet, against which they could have done nothing. Another miracle was Bonaparte's return to France without meeting the enemy's cruisers. Very often on this long and perilous voyage he

narrowly escaped capture. And what would his two
frigates and two despatch-boats have done against
the English fleet? The four old-fashioned Venetian
crafts were slow sailers that would have been over-
hauled in a few hours, and would have been power-
less against the finest ships in the world. Bonaparte's
only chance lay in not meeting the English ships, and
they were active on the Egyptian coast, and, indeed,
throughout the Mediterranean. The wind at first
drove the four vessels to the left of Alexandria, in
sight of the Cyrenaic coast, a hundred leagues from
Sidney Smith. Then they sailed to the northwest
and were detained twenty-four days off that arid and
uninhabited coast, where no one suspected their presence. Bonaparte ordered Admiral Gantheaume to
hug the African shore in order that he might tarry
in case of an attack by the English, and then with a
handful of men and the petty sum of seventeen thousand francs, which was the sole treasure he brought
from Egypt, he would make his way to Tunis or
Oran, and there again take shipping. September 15,
the wind changed and blew fresh from the southwest,
and they availed themselves of it. September 19,
they were running between Cape Bon and Sicily, a
dangerous place, because it was always full of English
ships. Fortunately they arrived there at nightfall;
had they got there earlier, the enemy would have
seen them; later, it would have been too dark to risk
pushing on. The four ships thus favored by fate
continued on their way, and after seeing in the dark·

ness the lights of an English cruiser, were out of sight at sunrise the next morning. A favorable wind brought them off Ajaccio.

Was Corsica still in possession of the French? Bonaparte did not know; and if he were to land there, he might be captured. He hesitated, and one of the despatch-boats hailed a fishing-smack and ascertained that Corsica still belonged to France. The fishermen could not say whether Provence was free or invaded by the Austrians, so Bonaparte decided to land in Corsica and find out the state of affairs. At that moment a ship sailed out of the harbor of Ajaccio; when it heard that Bonaparte was so near, it saluted him with all its guns, and hastened back to carry the news to the people of the town. At once there was firing of cannon, and soldiers, citizens, workmen, and peasants hastened to the water's edge; the sea was covered with boats that had put forth to meet the famous Corsican.

In one of these boats was an old woman, dressed in black, who stretched out her arms to the great man, rapturously exclaiming, "Caro figlio!" It was his nurse. Without stopping for quarantine, which was relaxed in his case, he landed and visited the house in which he was born; and as if he were already a sovereign, he administered justice and freed prisoners.

For the next few days contrary winds prevailed. For nine days Bonaparte was compelled to linger in Corsica, in continual fear lest the English should get wind of his presence. At last, October 7, the wind was fair, and he decided to sail for the coast of Provence, in spite of every obstacle; so they heaved and set forth, the *Muiron* being towed to sea by a boatful of sturdy rowers.

Bonaparte must have had his fill of strong emotions. The nearer he came to port, the more his danger grew. In a few hours, in a few minutes, he might be in the hands of the English; everything depended on the wind. Once on French soil, nothing could mar his future; but if he should fail to reach it, — if after abandoning his army in Egypt he should be captured by the English, — what would not his enemies say about his wild adventure? On one side ridicule, on the other omnipotence; to be branded as an adventurer, or to be glorified as a hero. This hardy gambler, who was forever playing at high stakes with fate, and so far had always won, liked these extreme crises, which fed his ardent imagination and fearless nature. During the whole day, October 7, they sailed along smoothly; already Bonaparte and his companions could see the mountains of Provence, and were congratulating themselves on landing in a few hours, when suddenly a lookout called down from aloft that he saw many sails, six leagues off, lit up by the sunset. Evidently they were the enemy's ships; and they all thought themselves lost. Gantheaume declared that Bonaparte's only chance was to jump into the boat that was towing the *Muiron* and to return to Ajaccio; but he quickly an-

swered the admiral: "Do you think I could consent
to run away like a criminal when fortune deserts me?
I am not destined to be captured and killed here.
. . . Your advice might be of use as a last resource,
after exchanging a few shots, when there is absolutely
no other means of escaping." It was his fatalism
that gave the hero of the Pyramids this imperturba-
bility, and his instinct did not deceive him. Suddenly he restored confidence to the whole crew; he
bade them notice that it was the sunset that lit up
the enemy's ships on the horizon, and that it left
*Muiron* and the *Carrière* in darkness. "We see
them, and they don't see us; so take courage!"
Does it not seem as if the winds obeyed him and
blew as he commanded, and that the sun, too, obeyed
him when it lit up the English fleet and hid in darkness the ship that bore the future Cæsar? "Away
with fears and cowardly counsels! Crowd on sail!"
shouted Bonaparte. "All hands aloft! Head north-
west!" The whole crew recovered confidence. They
made for the nearest anchorage, and the next morning, October 9, at nine o'clock, entered the bay of
Saint Raphael, eight hundred metres from the village
of that name, and half a league from Fréjus, after a
voyage of forty-four days.

Was Bonaparte going to submit to the quarantine?
He pretended that he was, but it was only a feint.
The quarantine station was about a half a mile
from Fréjus. An officer of the *Muiron* went ashore in
a small boat to announce Bonaparte's arrival, and

his intention to go into quarantine; but no sooner
was the officer seen, than the wildest excitement
broke out on the shore, which was soon covered with
a dense throng.   The people of Fréjus hastened into
their boats, crying, "Long live Bonaparte!" and
sailed out to the frigate on which he was.   "No
quarantine for you!" they shouted.   "We had rather
have the plague than the Austrians!   No quarantine
for our protector, for the hero who has come to defend Provence."   Bonaparte went ashore, and a
white horse was brought to him; he got on its back,
and entered Fréjus amid the cheers of the populace.
He stayed there only four hours, and then pushed
on, enjoying one long triumph.   At Aix, at Avignon,
at Valence, he was received with indescribable enthusiasm.   At Lyons he spent a day.   A huge crowd
gathered under his windows, calling upon him to
show himself.   In the evening he went to the theatre,
and hid in the back of the box, making Duroc sit in
front.   "Bonaparte, Bonaparte!" shouted the excited
audience, and so hotly, that he was forced to show
himself: at the moment he appeared the wildest
applause broke out.   At midnight he started again,
and instead of going through Mâcon, as was expected,
he took the road by the Bourbonnais, in a post-chaise
which pushed on swiftly night and day.

Paris had already received word by the telegraph
of his landing.   Within a fortnight information had
been received of Masséna's victory in Switzerland; of
Brune's in Holland; of Bonaparte's at Aboukir, and

of his arrival in France, and the joy universal. The bells were rung in every town and village through which he passed. At night bonfires were lit along the road. In the Paris theatres the actors announced the good news from the stage, and the plays were interrupted by cries and cheers and patriotic songs. In the Council of the Ancients, Lucien Bonaparte, though the youngest member, was elected President. When the news came that the hero of the Pyramids was returning, there were Republicans and patriots who were beside themselves with pleasure. It was when dining at the Luxembourg with Gohier, the President of the Directory, October 10, that Josephine heard that her husband had landed. She noticed that the news caused her host more surprise than pleasure. "Mr. President," she said, "do not be afraid that Bonaparte is coming with any intentions unfavorable to liberty. But you must unite to prevent his falling into bad company. I shall go to meet him. I must not on any account let any of his brothers, who hate me, see him first. Besides," she added, turning a look to Gohier's wife, "I need not fear calumny, when Bonaparte hears that you have been my most intimate friend; and he will be both pleased and grateful when he hears how well I have been treated here during his absence." Thus reassuring herself, Josephine at once left Paris to meet her husband; but since she took the road through Burgundy, and he the one through the Bourbonnais, she failed to meet him on the way, and he was back in Paris first.

## XXVI.

BONAPARTE arrived in Paris the morning of the 24th Vendémiaire, Year VIII. (October 16, 1799). He went at once to his house in the rue de la Victoire, and alone, as he did after his return from Italy. But then he knew that he would not find Josephine there, whereas now he felt sure that she would be there. The empty house filled him with bitterness. Where was his wife? Was she guilty, and did she dread to meet her enraged husband? Was everything that had been said about her true? Bonaparte's suspicious heart was full of wrath. His brothers, who were extremely hostile to Josephine, less from zeal for morality than from envy of her influence, skilfully fed this feeling of jealousy and anger. Bonaparte, who was deeply distressed already, began to think of separation and divorce. His old love, rekindled by his annoyance and fury, tortured him again. For a moment, he forgot the supreme power he was about to grasp, and thought only of his conjugal infelicity.

Josephine, too, was uneasy. She had tried to meet her husband to anticipate the accusations that would

be made against her. Confident of the power of her
beauty, she had said to herself: " Let me be the first
to see him, and he will fall into my arms." But she
had not been able to meet him on the way; and he
when he arrived had found a solitude. What must
he have thought in the empty rooms? He had been
there two days when Josephine reached Paris. She
trembled with anxiety. What was going to happen?
Was she to see a lover's or a judge's face confronting
her? Was she to meet the Bonaparte of other days,
so loving and affectionate, or a Bonaparte angry,
black, and terrible? It was a cruel uncertainty, full
of anguish. Poor woman! She was full of joy and
of uneasiness, uncertain whether she was to find
happiness or misery. Swiftly she ascended the little
staircase leading to her husband's room, but, to her
grief, the door was locked. She knocked; it was
not opened. She knocked again, and called, and
begged. He, protected by the bolts, answered
from within that the door would never again be
opened for her. Then she fell on her knees and
wept. The whole house was filled with her sobs.
She prayed and implored, but in vain. The night
wore on; she remained at the threshold of the forbidden room, which was a sort of paradise lost. She
did not lose all hope; her entreaties and tears did
not cease. Are not tears a woman's last argument?
Were not those tears to be dried by kisses? She
could not believe that after having been so much
adored, she would not be able to regain her empire.

Bonaparte might resist her voice when he could not see her face, but he would not resist her tearful smile. When she seemed in the deepest despair, Josephine still hoped, and with reason.

Yet she had long to wait; Bonaparte was so inflexible that at one moment she thought of ceasing the struggle. She was about to withdraw, exhausted by fatigue and emotion, when it occurred to one of her women to say to her, "Send for your son and daughter." She followed this wise advice. Eugene and Hortense came, and added their entreaties to Josephine's. " I beg of you. . . . Do not abandon our mother. . . . It will kill her. And we, poor orphans, whose father perished on the scaffold, shall we also lose him whom Providence put in his place?"

Bonaparte at last consented to open his door. His face was still severe; he uttered reproaches, and Josephine trembled. Turning to Eugene he said, " As for you, you shall not suffer for your mother's misdeeds; I shall keep you with me." "No, General," answered the young man; "I bid you farewell on the spot." Bonaparte began to yield; he pressed Eugene to his heart, and seeing both Josephine and Hortense on their knees, he forgave, and with eyes bright with joy, let himself be convinced by Josephine's arguments. The reconciliation was complete. At seven in the morning he sent for his brother Lucien, who had brought the charges, and when Lucien entered the room, he found the husband and wife reconciled and lying in the same bed.

Bonaparte did wisely in thus making a reconciliation with his wife. A separation would have been
a choice bit of scandal for the ill-disposed Royalists
to turn to their profit. Bonaparte was not yet a
Cæsar; his wife might be suspected. Besides, according to the tenets of society under the Directory, suspicions of that sort were not fatal to a fashionable
woman, and public opinion had more serious questions to consider, than whether Citizeness Bonaparte
had been, or had not been, faithful to her husband.
The hero of the Pyramids did the best thing possible
when he thus put an end to the not wholly disin-
terested accusations of his brothers, and turned his
attention to more serious matters than the recrimina-
tions of a husband who, rightly or wrongly, thought
himself deceived. Josephine was once more to further her husband's plans. She was bright, tactful,
and perfectly familiar with Parisian society and the
political world. Knowing all about everything, she
was about to play, with consummate skill, her part
in preparing for the *coup d'état* of Brumaire.

As soon as he arrived, Bonaparte became conscious
of the distrust of the Directory. The very first day
he went to the Luxembourg with Monge, a friend of
Gohier, the President of the Directory. "How glad
I am, my dear President," said Monge, "to find the
Republic triumphant!" "I too am very glad," said
Bonaparte, in some embarrassment. "The news we
received in Egypt was so alarming, that I did not
hesitate to leave my army to come to share its perils."

"General," answered Gohier, "they were great, but we have made a happy issue. You have come just in time to celebrate the glorious victories of your companions-in-arms." The next day, the 25th Vendémiaire, Bonaparte made another visit to the Directory. "Citizen Directors," he exclaimed, touching the handle of his sword, "I swear that this sword shall never be drawn except in defence of the Republic and of its government." Gohier replied: "General, your presence revives in every Frenchman's heart the glorious feeling of liberty. It is with shouts of 'Long live the Republic!' that Bonaparte ought to be received." The ceremony terminated with the fraternal embrace, but it was neither given nor received in a spirit of brotherly love.

The moment of the crisis drew near. Where was Bonaparte to find support? Among the zealous revolutionists, or on the side of the moderate? The head of the moderate party was one of the Directors, — Sieyès. For this former abbé he had an instinctive repulsion; but on reflection he felt that he needed him, and he decided to make use of him. Moreau, who had won celebrity by his victories, might be his rival; he conciliated him. Gohier has described their interview. He had invited to dinner Bonaparte, Josephine, and Sieyès. When Josephine saw the last-named in the drawing-room, "What have you done?" she asked Gohier; "Sieyès is the man whom Bonaparte detests more than any one. He can't endure him." In fact, during the whole dinner,

Bonaparte did not once speak to Sieyès; he even pretended not to see him. Sieyès was furious when he rose from the table. " Did you notice," he asked his host, "how the insolent fellow treated a member of the board which ought to have ordered him to be shot?"

After dinner Moreau arrived. It was the first time the two distinguished generals had met, and each seemed delighted to see the other. It was Bonaparte who made all the advances. A few days later he gave to Moreau, as a token of friendship, a sabre set with diamonds, and on the 18th Brumaire he was able to persuade him to be the jailer of the Directors who would not aid the *coup d'état*.

Madame Bonaparte was always of service to her husband in his relations with the men of whom he wanted to make use. She fascinated every one who came near her, by her exquisite grace and charming courtesy. All the brusqueness and violence of Bonaparte's manners were tempered by the soothing and insinuating gentleness of his amiable and kindly wife. She was to exercise direct influence on the victims and accomplices of the *coup d'état*, — on Barras, Gohier, Sieyès, Fouchè, Moreau, and Talleyrand. Who knows? Without Josephine's skill and tact, Bonaparte might, perhaps, have made a failure, have broken prematurely with Barras, have thrown off the mask too soon, before he had had time to make a formidable plot. The 8th Brumaire (October 30), when dining with Barras, he had great difficulty in restraining himself. Barras played the same game that he did, and spoke of his unselfishness, his fatigue, his shattered health, his need of rest, and said that he must resign and have a wholly unknown person, General Hedouville, put at the head of the govern-ment. Bonaparte was on the point of breaking out. He left Barras's rooms in a rage, and before going from the Luxembourg, went into those of Sieyès. "It's with you, and with you alone, that I mean to march," he said, and it was agreed to have everything ready for the 18th or 20th Brumaire.

Meanwhile Bonaparte became more crafty than ever. He said he was tired of men and things, that he was ill and quite upset by changing a dry climate for a damp one ; he posed for a Cincinnatus anxious to return to the plough, and kept out of the eyes of the public, arousing its curiosity the less he gratified it. If he went to the theatre, it was without giving notice, and he took a close box. He dressed more simply than usual. Instead of a full uniform or epaulettes, he wore the gray overcoat which was destined to become a subject of legend. He affected to prefer to anything else scientific or literary con-versation with his colleagues of the Institute. The austere Gohier, who was naturally credulous, and, besides, deceived by Josephine, refused to believe in any lawless plans on the part of such a man. Him-self a patriot and a Republican, he imagined that every one agreed with him regarding the Constitu-tion of the Year III. as the holy ark. All this time

he was weaving his political plans as if he were forming a plan for a battle. Every party regarded him as
its mainstay, and every party was mistaken. Bonaparte meant to make use of one of them, perhaps of
all, but not to be of service to any one of them. As
he said afterwards to Madame de Rémusat, in talking
about this period of his career: "The Directory was
not uneasy at my return; I was extremely on my
guard, and never in my life have I displayed more
skill. I saw the Abbé Sieyès, and promised him the
carrying out of his long-winded constitution; I received the leaders of the Jacobins, the agents of the
Bourbons; I gave my advice to every one, but I only
gave what would further my plans. I kept aloof
from the populace because I knew that it was time;
curiosity would make every one dog my steps. Every
one ran into my traps, and when I became the head
of the State, there was not a party in France that did
not base its hopes on my success."

The hour was approaching when there was to be
realized the wish, the prediction, which Suleau had
made in 1792, in the ninth number of his paper which
he published among Condé's soldiers at Coblentz. "I
repeat it calmly that the tutelary deity whom I in-
voke for my country is a despot, provided that he be
a man of genius. It is the absolute inflexibility of a
Richelieu that I demand; a man like that needs only
territory and force to create an empire. France can
be made a nation again only after it has been bowed in
silence beneath the iron rule of a severe and relentless

master. When I call on despotism to come to the aid of my unhappy country, I mean the union of powers in the hands of an imperious master, of a cruel capacity, jealous of rule, and utterly absolute. I demand a magnanimous usurper who knows how, by means of the haughty and brilliant spirit of a Cromwell, to make a people admired and respected, whom he compels to respect and bless their subjection." This issue was about to appear. The long plot framed by the reaction since 1795 was finished.

# XXVII.

A FEW days before the 18th Brumaire, Bona-parte happened to be at the estate of his brother Joseph, at Mortefontaine. Being anxious for a free discussion with Regnault de Saint Jean d'Angély, of the events that were preparing, he proposed to him that they should take a ride together. As the two men were galloping wildly by the ponds, over the rocks, Bonaparte's horse stumbled on a stone hidden in the sand and threw the general off with some violence to a distance of twelve or fifteen feet. Regnault sprang from his horse and ran up to him, finding him senseless: his pulse was imperceptible; he did not breathe; he thought him dead. It was a false alarm. In a few minutes Bonaparte came to himself, with no bones broken, no scratch, no bruise, and mounted his horse. "Oh, General," exclaimed his companion, "what a fright you gave me!" and Bonaparte said, "That was a little stone on which all our plans came near shattering." It was true; that pebble might have changed the fate of the world.

The conspiracy was organized, and the end was approaching. Bonaparte, who was a conspirator as well as a soldier, prepared it with thoroughly Italian subtlety and wiliness. With consummate skill he anticipated public opinions, while pretending aversion to the *coup d'état* which was his heart's desire. For several days the officers in Paris had been trying to get an opportunity to present their respects, but he had not consented to see them. The officers complained, and the public began to say, " He won't do any more than he did after his return from Italy. Who will help us out of the mire ? " To the end he haunted Republican society. Josephine and he were untiring in their attentions to Gohier and his wife. At the same time he understood how to call up memories of the Terror, to impress men's imaginations, and to evoke the red spectre which always made the blood of the middle classes run cold.

As Edgar Quinet has put it, the 18th Brumaire was to be a union of fear and glory. Every one was anxious and in terror of worse things yet, — of riots, proscriptions, the guillotine, — and sure that no one but Bonaparte could prevent the return of 1793. He was entreated to take some step, and when he complied, he seemed to be yielding to popular clamor. The *coup d'état* was in the air. Everywhere Bonaparte found allies and accomplices. To secure general approval only one thing was wanted, — success.

The 15th Brumaire (the final plan of the conspiracy was to be determined on that day), Bonaparte was present at a subscription dinner given him by five or six hundred members of the two Councils. "Never at a civic banquet," says Gohier in his Memoirs, "was there less expression given to Republican sentiments." There was no gaiety, no mutual congratulations. The dinner was given in the Temple of Victory, otherwise known as the Church of Saint Sulpice. It seemed as if no one dared to speak aloud in the sanctuary, and as if every one were oppressed by some gloomy foreboding. Every one was watching and knowing that he was watched. Bonaparte, who sat at the right hand of Gohier, the President of the Directory, appeared out of spirits and ill at ease. He partook of nothing but bread and wine brought to him by his aide-de-camp. Was he afraid of poison? The official toasts, proposed without enthusiasm, were drunk coolly. Bonaparte did not even stay till the end of the dinner; he suddenly rose from the table, walked about, uttering a few hasty words to the principal guests, and went away.

Arnault describes that evening at the general's house. Josephine did the honors of her drawing-room with even more than her usual grace. Men of all parties were gathered there, — generals, deputies, Royalists, Jacobins, abbés, a minister, and even the President of the Directory. From the lordly air of the master of the house, it seemed as if already he felt himself to be a monarch surrounded by his court. Minister Fouché arrived and sat down on the sofa by Madame Bonaparte's side.

" *Gohier.* What's the news, Citizen Minister?

" *Fouché.* The news? Oh! nothing.

" *Gohier.* But besides that?

" *Fouché.* Always the same idle rumors.

" *Gohier.* What?

" *Fouché.* The same old conspiracy.

" *Gohier (shrugging his shoulders).* The conspiracy!

" *Fouché.* Yes, the conspiracy! But I know how to treat that. I thoroughly understand it, Citizen Director; have confidence in me; I am not going to be caught. If there had been a conspiracy all the time it's been talked of, would there not be some signs of it in the Place de la Révolution or in the plain of Grenelle? [At these words Fouché burst out laughing.]

" *Madame Bonaparte.* For shame, Citizen Fouché! Can you laugh at such things?

" *Gohier.* The Minister speaks like a man who understands his business. But calm yourself, Citizeness; to talk about such things before ladies is to think they will not have to be done. Act like the government; do not be uneasy at those rumors. Sleep quietly."

Bonaparte listened with a smile.

The evening passed as usual; there was no excitement, no uneasiness on any one's face. Her drawing-room gradually emptied. Fouché and Gohier took leave of Josephine, who withdrew to her own room. Arnault stayed to the last and had this conversation with Bonaparte.

"General, I have come to know if to-morrow is still the day, and to get your instructions."

"It's put off till the 18th."

" Till the 18th ? "

"The 18th."

" When it has got out? Don't you notice how every one is talking about it ? "

" Everybody is talking about it, but no one believes in it. Besides, there is a reason. Those imbeciles of the Council of the Ancients have scruples. They have begged for twenty-four hours for reflection ! "

" And you have granted them ? "

"What's the harm? I give them time to convince themselves that I can do without them what I wish to do with them. To the 18th, then. Come in and drink a cup of tea to-morrow; if there is any change, I'll let you know. Good night."

Two days were not too many for the final preparations. "Josephine was in the secret," says General de Ségur. "Nothing was concealed from her. In every conference at which she was present her discretion, her gentleness, her grace, and the ready ingenuity of her delicate and cool intelligence were of great service. She justified Bonaparte's renewed confidence in her."

The 16th and 17th, Bonaparte and his adherents completed the elaboration of their programme, which was simple and ingenious. A provision of the Constitution, that of the Year III., authorized the Council of Ancients, in case of peril for the Republic, to convoke the Legislative Body (the Council of Ancients and the Council of Five Hundred) outside of the capital, to preserve it from the influence of the multitude, and to choose a general to command the troops destined to defend the legislature. The Constitution also provided that from the moment when this change of the place of meeting was voted by the Council of Ancients, all discussion on the part of the two councils was forbidden until the change was made. This was the corner-stone on which the conspiracy was to build. The alleged public peril was a so-called Jacobin conspiracy, which, according to Bonaparte's partisans, threatened the Legislative Body. The 18th Brumaire was set for the day when the Council of Ancients should vote to change the place of meeting to Saint Cloud, and Bonaparte should be assigned the command of the troops. The Council was to be convoked at the Tuileries, where it always met, at eight in the morning; some one should take the floor and enlarge on the perils of the so-called Jacobin plot, and, the vote to change the place of meeting once carried, the Council of Five Hundred, which did not meet till eleven, would have to submit in silence.

But how collect the troops about Bonaparte in the morning before the vote was taken? and to succeed, he needed their presence at the very beginning.

The 17th Division, with its headquarters in Paris, was not under his orders. He was not Minister of War, and had no command. How was it possible, without exciting suspicion, to assemble, under the very eyes of the government, the forces that were about to overthrow it? What pretext could be devised for gathering a staff in the house in the rue de la Victoire, and regiments about the Tuileries? For many days the officers of the Army of Paris and the National Guard had been desirous of presenting their respects to General Bonaparte. It was decided that he should receive them at his house, at six in the morning, the 18th Brumaire; and this untimely hour was accounted for by a journey on which it was pretended that the general was about to depart. Three regiments of cavalry had sought the honor of riding by him. Word was sent that he would receive them at seven o'clock in the morning of the same day. To go from the rue de la Victoire to the Tuileries he needed a cavalry escort; word was sent to one of his most devoted adherents, a Corsican, Colonel Sébastiani, who was invited to be on horseback at five in the morning, with two hundred dragoons of his regiment, the 9th. Sébastiani, without waiting for orders from his superiors, at once accepted this mission. With a brilliant staff of generals and mounted officers, preceded and followed by an escort of dragoons, Bonaparte would ride in the morning to the Tuileries at the very moment that the change of the place of meeting should have been voted by the Council of Ancients; he would receive command of the garrison of Paris and its suburbs, and be ordered to protect the two Councils, who should sit the next day, the 19th, at Saint Cloud. In the course of the 18th Barras would be persuaded to hand in his resignation. This, following close on the heels of the resignation of Sieyès and Roger-Ducos, would disorganize the Directory, which, consisting of but two members, Moulins and Gohier, would be kept under guard at the Luxembourg by General Moreau, and would give way to a new government, which had its constitution all ready, with Napoleon for its head. It was hoped that the Council of Five Hundred would not oppose their plans, and that the revolution, which assumed an appearance of legality, would be accomplished without violence. In any case, Bonaparte would go on to the end. If the Five Hundred refused their approval, he resolved to proceed without it. The snares were set. The legislature was to fall into them. Every preparation had been made. The conspirators bade one another farewell till the morrow.

# XXVIII.

## THE 18TH BRUMAIRE.

A T five in the morning, Sébastiani, the colonel
of the 9th Dragoons, had occupied the garden
of the Tuileries and the Place de la Révolution with
eight hundred men. He himself had taken a place
with two hundred mounted dragoons before Bonaparte's house in the rue de la Victoire. At six,
arrived Lefebvre, the commander of the military
division. Orders had been sent to different regiments without saying anything to him, and he was
surprised to see Sébastiani's dragoons, but Bonaparte
was in no way disconcerted. "Here," he said, "is
the Turkish sabre which I carried at the battle of the
Pyramids. Do you, who are one of the most valiant
defenders of the country, accept it? Will you let our
country perish in the hands of the pettifoggers who
are ruining it?" Lefebvre, wild with joy, exclaimed,
"If that's what's up, I am ready. We must throw
those pettifoggers into the river at once." The house
and garden were speedily filled with officers in full
uniform. Only one was in citizen's dress; it was
Bernadotte. Resisting Bonaparte's offers, he said,

"No! no! you will fail. I am going away where perhaps I shall be able to save you."

Eight o'clock struck; a woman entered; it was Madame Gohier, wife of the President of the Directory. The evening before, her husband had received this note, brought by Eugene de Beauharnais : —

"17th Brumaire, Year VIII.

"My DEAR GOHIER : Won't you and your wife breakfast with us to-morrow at eight. Do not fail us ; there are a good many interesting things I should like to talk to you about. Good by, my dear Gohier.

"Believe me always

"Sincerely yours,

"LA PAGERIE-BONAPARTE."

The early hour aroused Gohier's suspicions. He told his wife : "You will go; but you must tell Madame Bonaparte that I can't accept her invitation, but that I shall have the honor of seeing her in the course of the morning."

When Bonaparte saw Madame Gohier arrive alone, he frowned.

" What ! " he exclaimed, " isn't the President coming ? "

"No, General, he couldn't possibly come."

"But he must come. Write him a line, Madame, and I will see that the note is sent."

" I will write to him, General, but I have servants here who will take charge of the letter."

Madame Gohier took a pen and wrote to her hus-band as follows : —

" You did well not to come, my dear : everything convinces me that the invitation was a snare. I shall come to you as soon as possible."

When Madame Gohier had sent this note, Madame Bonaparte came to her, and said : " Everything you see must indicate to you, Madame, what has got to happen. I can't tell you how sorry I am that Gohier did not accept the invitation which I had planned with Bonaparte, who wants the President of the Directory to be one of the members of the govern-ment which he proposes to establish. By sending my son with the note, I thought that I indicated the importance I attached to it."

" I am going to join him, Madame; my presence is superfluous here."

" I shall not detain you. When you see your hus-band, bid him reflect, and do you yourself reflect on the wish I have been authorized to express to you. . . . Use all your influence, I beg of you, to induce him to come."

Madame Gohier returned to the Luxembourg, leav-ing Bonaparte amid the officers of all grades who were to help him in the *coup d'état.*

What was going on at the Tuileries meanwhile? The Council of Ancients met at eight o'clock. Cor-net took the floor, and began to speak about con-spiracy, daggers, Terrorists. " If the Council of Ancients does not protect the country and liberty from the greatest dangers that have ever threatened it, the fire will spread. . . . It will be impossible to stop its devouring progress. The country will be consumed. . . . Representatives of the people, ward off this dreadful conflagration, or the Republic will cease to exist, and its skeleton will be in the talons of vultures who will dispute its fleshless limbs!"

This declamatory outburst produced a distinct effect. The Council of Ancients, in accordance with articles of the Constitution authorizing, in case of public peril, a change in the place of meeting of the Legislative Body, passed the following votes : —

" Article 1. The Legislative Body is transferred to the Commune of Saint Cloud ; the two Councils will sit there in the two wings of the palace.

" Article 2. They will meet there at noon to-morrow, the 19th Brumaire. All official acts and deliberations are forbidden at any place, before that hour.

" Article 3. General Bonaparte is charged with the execution of this decree. . . . The general commanding the 17th military division, the Guard of the Legislative Body, the stationary National Guard, the troops of the line now in the Commune of Paris, are hereby placed under his orders.

" Article 4. General Bonaparte is summoned to the Council to receive a copy of this decree and to take oath accordingly."

Scarcely had the vote been taken when Cornet hastened off to tell Bonaparte in the rue de la Victoire.

It was about nine o'clock.  The general was addressing his officers from the steps of his house, "The
Republic is in danger; we must come to its aid."
After he had read the vote of the Ancients, he
shouted, "Can I depend on you to save the Republic?"  Cheers were their answer.  Then he got on
his horse, and, followed by a brilliant escort, among
whom were noticed Moreau, Macdonald, Lefebvre,
Berthier, Lannes, Beurnonville, Marmont, Murat, he
rode to the Tuileries.  Sébastiani's dragoons opened
and closed the way.

There were but few people about the Tuileries, for
most had no idea of what was going to happen.  The
gates of the garden, which was full of troops, were
closed.  The weather was very fine; the sun lit up
the helmets and bayonets.  Bonaparte rode through
the garden, and, alighting in front of the Pavilion
of the Clock, appeared before the Council of Ancients, the door being opened to him.

"Citizen Representatives," he said, "the Republic
was about to perish; your vote has saved it!  Woe to
those who dare to oppose its execution!  Aided by
my comrades, I shall know how to resist their efforts.
It is vain that precedents are sought in the past to dis-
turb your minds.  There is in all history nothing like
the eighteenth century, and nothing in the century is
like its end.  We desire the Republic; we desire it
founded on true liberty, on the representative system.
We shall have it; I swear this in my own name and
in that of my fellow-soldiers."

Only one deputy observed that in this oath no mention was made of the Constitution. The President, wishing to spare Bonaparte too open perjury, silenced him and closed the meeting.

Bonaparte went down into the garden again and reviewed the troops, who cheered him warmly.

It was eleven o'clock, the hour set for the meeting of the Council of Five Hundred. The Deputies heard with indignation the vote of the Ancients, but their President, Lucien Bonaparte, silenced them. The Constitution was imperative; all discussion was forbidden. They had nothing to do but to agree to meet at Saint Cloud the next day.

Of the five Directors, two, Sieyès and Roger-Ducos, had already handed in their resignations; the third, Barras, at the request of Bruix and Talleyrand, had just followed their example, and had started for his estate, Grosbois; the other two, Gohier and Moulins, made one final effort. They went to the Tuileries, and found Bonaparte in the hall of the Inspectors of the Council of Ancients. After a lively altercation, they returned to the Luxembourg, having accomplished nothing.

A few moments before, Bonaparte had spoken thus to Bottot, Barras's secretary : " What have you done with this France that I left so full of glory? I left peace; I find war! I left you victorious; I find you in defeat! I left you the millions of Italy; I find everywhere ruinous laws and misery! . . . What have you done with the hundred thousand Frenchmen whom I knew, the companions of my glory? They are dead! This state of things cannot last. In three years it would lead to despotism."

In her *Considerations on the French Revolution*, Madame de Staël says: " Bonaparte worked to make his predictions true. Would it not be a great lesson for the human race, if these Directors were to rise from their graves and demand of Napoleon an account for the boundary of the Rhine and the Alps which the Republic had conquered, an account for the foreigner who twice entered Paris, and for the Frenchmen who perished from Cadiz to Moscow?"

But who on the 18th Brumaire could predict these future disasters? Bonaparte's soldiers imagined themselves forever invincible. The military spirit was triumphant. No more red caps, but the grenadiers' hats; no more pikes, but bayonets. The Jacobins had lived their day. The furious diatribes of the Club du Manège called forth no echo. The terrible Santerre was a mere harmless brewer. The faubourgs had grown calm. The roll of the drum had silenced the voice of the tribunes. Even the men of the old régime were fascinated by the career of arms. This is what a young aristocrat said, who was one day to be General de Ségur, the historian of the exploits of the grand army: —

" It was the very moment when Napoleon, summoned by the Council of Ancients, began in the Tuileries the revolution of the 18th Brumaire and was haranguing the garrison of Paris to secure it against

the other Council.   The garden gate stopped me.   I
leaned against it, and gazed on the memorable scene.
Then I ran around the enclosure, trying every entrance; at last I reached the gate near the draw-
bridge, and saw it open.   A regiment of dragoons
came out, the 9th; they started for Saint Cloud, with
their overcoats rolled up, helmets on their heads,
sabres in hand, and with the warlike excitement, the
fierce and determined air of soldiers advancing on
the enemy to conquer or die.   At this sight, all the
soldier's blood I had inherited from all my ancestors
boiled in my veins.   My career was determined.
From that moment I was a soldier; I thought of
nothing but battles, and despised every other career."

Madame de Staël records that on the 18th Brumaire she happened to arrive in Paris from Switzerland.   When changing horses at some leagues from
the city, she heard that the Director Barras had just
passed by, escorted by gens d'armes.   "The postilions,"
she goes on, "gave us the news of the day, and this
way of hearing it made it only more vivid.   It was
the first time since the Revolution that one man's
name was in every mouth.   Previously they had said:
The Constituent Assembly has done this, or the
people, or the Convention; now nothing was spoken
of but this man who was going to take the place of
all.   That evening the city was excited with expectation of the morrow, and doubtless the majority of
peaceful citizens, fearing the return of the Jacobins,
then desired that General Bonaparte should succeed

My feelings, I must say, were mixed. When the fight had once begun, a momentary victory of the Jacobins might be the signal for bloodshed; but nevertheless the thought of Bonaparte's triumph filled me with a pain that might be called prophetic."

He himself, well contented with his day, returned to his house in the rue de la Victoire, where he found Josephine happy and confident. All the military preparations were complete : Moreau occupied the Luxembourg. Lannes, the Tuileries ; Sérurier, the Point du Jour; Murat, the palace of Saint Cloud. Bonaparte fell asleep as calmly as on the eve of a great battle.

## XXIX.

THE revolution which Bonaparte effected is called the 18th Brumaire, yet in fact the 18th Brumaire was a mere prelude; the decisive day was the 19th. On the 18th respect was paid to the law; on the 19th the law was violated, and for that reason the conqueror, desiring to excuse himself before history, chose the 18th as the official date of the revolution.

The night passed quietly; the faubourgs did not dare to rise. The people of Paris looked on what was happening as if it were an interesting play which aroused no emotion or wrath.

The morning of the 19th saw the road from Paris to Saint Cloud crowded with troops, carriages, and a throng full of curiosity. Bonaparte's success was predicted, but the issue was not yet certain, and thus the public interest was all the more excited. It had been decided that both Councils should meet at noon. The Representatives were punctual, and a little before twelve o'clock Bonaparte was on horseback, opposite the palace of Saint Cloud, at the head of his troops. The Ancients were to meet on the first floor in the Gallery of Apollo, full of Mignard's decorations, and the Five Hundred in the orange house; but the preparations were not completed at the appointed hour, and it was not till two that the sessions began. While waiting, the deputies strolled in the park. It was evident that the Five Hundred were distinctly unfavorable to Bonaparte. He, much annoyed by the delay, kept going and coming, giving repeated orders, betraying the utmost impatience.

At two, the sessions of the Councils were opened. That of the Ancients began with unimportant preliminaries; that of the Five Hundred, with an outbreak of passion. Lucien Bonaparte presided. Gardin proposed that a committee of seven be appointed to make a report on the measures to be taken in behalf of the public safety. Hostile murmurs made themselves heard. Delbel called out from his seat: "The Constitution before everything! The Constitution or death! Bayonets do not frighten us; we are free here!" A formidable clamor arose: "No dictatorship! Down with dictators!" Grandmaison moved that all the members of the Council of Five Hundred should be at once compelled to renew their oath of fidelity to the Constitution of the Year III. The motion was carried amid great enthusiasm. The roll was called for each member to swear in turn. Lucien Bonaparte himself swore fidelity to the Constitution which he was about to destroy.

A letter was brought from Barras. Amid general

excitement, the secretary read aloud this letter, in which the Director announced his resignation; it ended thus: "The glory which accompanies the return of the illustrious warrior, for whom I had the honor of opening the way, the distinct marks of the confidence accorded him by the Legislative Body, and the decree of the National Representatives, have convinced me that whatever may be the part to which the public interests henceforth may summon me, the dangers to liberty are surmounted and the interests of the army guaranteed. I return with joy to the ranks of private citizens, happy, after so many storms, to restore, uninjured and more deserving of respect than ever, the destinies of the Republic of which I have had in part the care."

This letter produced a feeling of angry surprise. Of the five Directors, three had resigned. The government was dissolved. Resistance to Bonaparte had nothing to stand on. Grandmaison said from the tribune: "First of all, we must know whether the resignation of Barras is not the result of the extraordinary circumstances in which we are placed. I think that among the members present there are some who know where we came from and whither we are going."

While the session of the Five Hundred began thus, what had been taking place among the Ancients? Bonaparte had just made his appearance there and had spoken as a master. "Citizen Representatives," he had said, "you are not now in ordinary conditions, but on the edge of a volcano. Already I and my fellow-soldiers are overwhelmed with abuse. People are talking of a new Cromwell, a new Cæsar. If I had desired to play such a part, I could easily have taken it when I returned from Italy. . . . Let us save the two things for which we have made so many sacrifices, — liberty and equality." And when a deputy interrupted with, " Speak about the Constitution," he answered : " The Constitution? you no longer have one. It is you who destroyed it by attacking, on the 18th Fructidor, the national representation ; by annulling, on the 22d Floréal, the popular elections ; by assaulting the independence of the government. All parties have striven to destroy this constitution of which you speak. They have all come to me to confide their plans and to induce me to aid them. I have refused; but if it is necessary, I will name the parties and the men." Then he mentioned Barras ; then the name of Moulins escaped him, but stormy contradictions followed this inexact statement.

Bonaparte, who was rather a man of action than a debater, was for a moment disconcerted. The tumult was growing; but he, abandoning persuasion, resorted to threats. Assuming the air of a protector who makes himself feared by those he guards, he said: "Surrounded by my companions in arms, I shall know how to aid you. I call to witness these brave grenadiers whose bayonets I see, and whom I have so often led against the enemy. If any orator, in the pay of foreigners, should speak of outlawing me, I shall summon my companions in arms. Remember that I march in the company of the God of fortune and of war." The Council of Ancients replied to this stormy outbreak by respectfully according to Bonaparte the honors of the meeting, and he left the hall and returned to his soldiers : he had a note taken to Josephine in which he told her to be calm, that all was going on well.

At the same time he heard of the outburst of passion in the Council of Five Hundred. Thereupon he ordered a company of grenadiers to follow him, and leaving it at the door of the Chamber, he crossed the threshold and stepped forward alone, hat in hand. It was just when Grandmaison was in the tribune speaking about Barras's letter. It was five in the afternoon; the lamps were lit. At the sight of Bonaparte the Five Hundred uttered a long cry of indignation : "Down with the Dictator! Down with the tyrant!" They all rushed to meet the general, crowding him and denouncing him; they forced him several steps back. Many brandished daggers and threatened his life. It was, he said later, the most perilous moment of his life. He was saved by Beauvais, a Norman deputy of enormous strength, who drove back his assailants and brought him to his soldiers, who were hastening to his aid. One of the soldiers, Grenadier Thomé, had his clothes cut by a dagger. The tumult was indescribable; the orange house was like a battle-field.

It was in vain that Lucien tried to support his brother. Cries arose: " Outlaw him. Down with Bonaparte and his accomplices! " His desk was over-run. " March, President," said a deputy ; " put to vote the proposition to outlaw him."

Lucien descended the steps, denounced on every side. " Go back to your place! Don't make us lose time! Put to vote the outlawry of the dictator!" " Tell my brother," he said " that I have been driven from my chair. Ask him for an armed force to pro-tect my departure." Frégeville ran to inform Gen-eral Bonaparte, who had just left the orange house, under the guard of his soldiers, and had got on his horse, telling the soldiers that he narrowly escaped assassination. The troops cheered their general and brandished their weapons. He had but a word to say, and the Five Hundred would be dispersed, but this word he hesitated to utter. He, who knew no fear, became confused, like Cæsar, as Lucan describes him, undecided at the Rubicon.

Meanwhile the tumult in the orange house was be-coming more intense. After two speeches, one from Bertrand of Calvados, the other from Talet, both hos-tile to Bonaparte, Lucien began to speak : " I do not rise," he said, " to make direct opposition to the motion [of outlawing Bonaparte] ; but it is a proper moment to remind the Council that the suspicions which have been brought up so lightly have pro-duced lamentable excesses. Can even an illegal step make us forget such noble deeds and important ser-

vice in behalf of the country!" Lucien was interrupted by continual murmurs. There were cries,
"Time is flying; put the motion!" "No," resumed
Lucien, "you cannot vote such a measure without
hearing the General; I ask that he be called to the
bar. . . . These unseasonable interruptions which
drown the voice of your colleagues are indecent.
They continue and become more violent. Then I
shall not insist. When order is once more established, and your extraordinary indecorum has ceased,
you will yourselves render justice where it is due,
without passion."

The uproar became so violent that Lucien could
not face the storm; so taking off his toga, and laying
it on the tribune, he said: "Liberty no longer exists
here. Since I have no means of making myself
heard, you will at least see your President, in token
of public grief, placing here the insignia of the public magistracy."

"It is a lamentable thing," says Edgar Quinet, in
his *Revolution*, "that this last Assembly, already
threatened, surrounded, denounced, with swords at
its throat, should have no other defence against the
soldiers' arms than such blunt weapons, — a conscience, new oaths, a roll-call, promises to die, uproar, and the vain protests with which an Assembly,
deserted by the nation at the hour of peril, deceives
despair and amuses its last hour. Then were there
moments of indescribable anxiety, when history lay
in the balance between two opposing destinies, liberty

knowing no way in which to save itself, and the general, averse to putting an end to the complications, not daring to make a violent usurpation."

After he had placed his toga on the edge of the tribune, Lucien ceased speaking. He saw the company of grenadiers which he had asked of his brother. To the officer in command, who said, " Citizen President, we are here by the General's orders," he replied in a loud voice, " We will follow you ; open a passage." Then turning to the Vice-President, he made a sign to him to close the meeting. Leaving the orange house, he hastened to the courtyard, where he found his brother motionless and silent, on horseback, surrounded by his soldiers. " Give me a horse," he shouted, "and sound the drums !" In a moment he was on the horse of one of the dragoons, and after a roll of the drums, which was followed by profound silence : " Citizen soldiers," he said angrily, " I announce to you that the vast majority of this Council is at this moment intimidated by a few representatives armed with daggers. The brigands, doubtless in English pay, desire to outlaw your general ! Being entrusted with the execution of the vote of the Ancients, against which they are in revolt, I appeal to the military. Citizen soldiers, save the representatives of the people from the representatives of daggers, and let the majority of the Council be delivered from the stiletto by bayonets ! Long live the Republic !" To this cry the soldiers an-

swered with " Long live Bonaparte ! "    And Lucien,
waving a sword, cried out, " I swear with this sword
to stab my own brother, if he ever does violence to
the liberty of the French ! "    The general hesitated
no longer.    He ordered the grenadiers commanded
by Murat and Leclerc to enter the Chamber of the
Five Hundred.    The drums were beaten ; their roar
drowned the voices of the representatives of the
people, as they had drowned the voice of Louis XVI.
In a moment the hall was empty, the deputies having
fled through the windows of the orange house into
the garden.    Only one clung to his seat, saying he
wished to die there.    They laughed at him, and at
last he took flight like the rest.

In Paris news was impatiently awaited.    At one
moment the rumor ran that Bonaparte was proscribed
and outlawed ; the next, that he was victorious and
had expelled the Five Hundred.    It is thus that Madame de Staël describes her different impressions
during this agitated day : " One of my friends who
was present at the sitting in Saint Cloud sent me
bulletins every hour.    Once he told me the Jacobins
were going to carry everything before them, and I
made ready to leave France again ; the next moment
I heard that Bonaparte had triumphed, the soldiers
having expelled the National Representatives, and I
wept, not over liberty, which never existed in France,
but over the hope of that liberty without which a
country knows only shame and misery."

All day Madame Bonaparte, the general's mother, had been very anxious, though outwardly calm. Three of her children were engaged in the struggle, and in case of Napoleon's failure, all three would be severely punished. Nevertheless, with her usual energy, she concealed her emotions. In the evening, when the definite result was still unknown, she was yet courageous enough to go with her daughters to the Théâtre Feydeau, the fashionable theatre, where the *Auteur dans son ménage* was given. In the course of the play some one stepped forward on the stage, and shouted out, "Citizens, General Bonaparte has just escaped being assassinated at Saint Cloud by traitors to this country!" Madame Leclerc screamed with terror. It was half-past nine o'clock. Then Madame Bonaparte and her daughters left the theatre and hastened to the rue de la Victoire, where they found Josephine, who reassured them.

The Bonaparte family had nothing more to fear. All resistance was impossible at Paris or at Saint Cloud. The soldiers of the man who was about to be the First Consul camped that night on the battle-field. At eleven o'clock he summoned his secretary: "I want the whole town, when it wakes up to-morrow, to think of nothing but me. Write!" And he dictated one of those showy proclamations which he knew so well how to compose for an effect upon the masses. He gave to the *coup d'état* a false appearance of legality. The two Councils had just met for a night session. Most of the Five Hundred were absent. But it made no difference; the minority was to be taken for a majority. Bonaparte, Sieyès, and Roger-Ducos were appointed consuls and were entrusted with the preparations of a new constitution, aided by two legislative commissions. Sixty-one deputies of the Five Hundred, guilty of having wished to make the law respected, were declared incapable for the future of serving as representatives. Lucien ended the night session with this speech: " French liberty was born in the tennis-court of Versailles. Since that immortal meeting it has dragged itself along till our time, the prey in turn of the inconsistency, the weakness, and the convulsive ailments of infancy. To-day it has assumed its manly robes. No sooner have you established it on the love and confidence of the French than the smile of peace and abundance shine on its lips. Representatives of the people, listen to the blessing of the people and of its armies, long the plaything of factions, and may their shouts reach the depths of your hearts ! Listen also to the sublime voice of posterity ! If liberty was born at the tennis-court of Versailles, it has been consolidated in the orange house of Saint Cloud. The Constituents of '89 were the fathers of the Revolution, but the legislators of the Year VIII. will be the fathers and peacemakers of the country." There is nothing in the world easier than to set what has succeeded in brilliant colors. In Brumaire, as in Fructidor, might had overcome right, and might never lacks worshippers. All was over ; the game had been won. At three in the morning Bonaparte got into his carriage and drove back from Saint Cloud to Paris, where the inhabitants had illuminated their houses, in celebration of his illegal victory.

# XXX.

BONAPARTE returned from Saint Cloud to Paris, between three and four in the morning, having in the carriage with him his brother Lucien, Sieyès, and General Gardanne. All the way he was absorbed, thoughtful, silent. Was it physical and moral fatigue following so many emotions? Was it a presentiment of the future, the thought of his future deeds, which were busying the imagination of this great historical character? What reflections he must have made on the turns of fortune! Had he been beaten, he would have been outlawed; as the conqueror, he knew no law but his own will. Beaten, he would have been an apostate, a renegade, a wretch; his laurels would have been dragged in the dust, and he himself would have been carted to the gibbet. As conqueror, he was to ascend the steps to the capitol, swearing that he was his country's saviour. Conquered, he would have been a vile Corsican, unworthy the name of Frenchman. As conqueror, he was the man of destiny, the protecting genius. Instead of abuse, he was to hear songs of praise, and to see the old parties laying down their arms; young Royalists enthusiastically joining him under the tricolored flag; the army and populace rending the air with their cheers; priests singing hymns; in the forum, the camp, the churches, — he was to find everywhere the same outburst of joy. Yet those who make the *coup d'état* know very well that the ovations which greet them depend solely on their success, and that their success depends on the merest trifles. Succeed, and you are a hero; fail, and you are a traitor. How ridiculous is human judgment, how vain and uncertain the verdict of history! Posterity, like universal suffrage, is forever altering its judgment. What is truth one year is false the next. The voice of the people is not the voice of God.

Bonaparte was back in the house in the rue de la Victoire, which had always brought him happiness, — where he was married, whence he started for Italy and Egypt, whither he always returned victorious, and where two days before he had felt confident of the success of the *coup d'état*, the origin of his supreme power. He kissed Josephine tenderly and told her all the incidents of the day, passing rapidly over the danger he had been through in the orange house, and jesting about the embarrassment which he, a man of action, felt when compelled to speak. Then he rested a few hours, and woke up in the morning, the master of Paris and of France.

Fate had spoken. Who could resist the man with whom marched "the God of fortune and of war"?

This is what is said by Edgar Quinet, the great democratic writer, who describes the passive adhesion of
the whole people: "This was, I imagine, the greatest
grief of the last representatives of liberty in France;
after which all grief is but a jest. They imagined
that they were followed by people whose souls they
owned. For many days they were going here and
there, peering into the cross-ways and public places.
Where were the magnificent orators at the bar of the
old assemblies? Where the forests of pikes so often
uplifted, and the repeated oaths of fourteen years,
and the magnanimous nation which the mere shade
of a master had so often driven wild with anger?
Where was their pride? Where the Roman indignation? How could those great hearts have fallen in
so few years? No echo answered. The Five Hundred found only astonished faces, sudden conversions
to force, incredulity, and silence. All was dissipated
in a moment; they themselves seemed to be pursuing
a vision."

The time was drawing nigh when republican simplicity was to give way to the formal and refined
etiquette of a monarchy; when the woman who languished in the prison of the Carmes, under the Terror,
was to be surrounded with the pomp and splendor of
an Asiatic queen; when Lucien Bonaparte was to
congratulate himself, as he said, that "he had not got
into the crowd of princes and princesses who were
taken in tow by all the renegades of the Republic."
For, he goes on, "who knows whether the example

of all these apostasies might not have perverted my political and philosophic sentiments ? "

The more one studies history, the more depressing it is. The illusions in which peoples indulge call forth a smile — illusions about liberty, about absolutism. Every government thinks itself immortal; not one, before its fall, sees the abyss yawning before it. If we compare the results and the efforts, we can only lament the vicious circle in which unhappy humanity forever turns. What would Bonaparte have said, what his admirers and officers, if any one had announced to them what the end of their epoch would be? And what did the Republicans, formerly so haughty and arrogant, think of their change of heart? France has paid a high price for these incessant apostasies. By dint of burning what she has adored, and adoring what she has burned, she has become distrustful of her own glories, ready to destroy the most illustrious legends of centuries, to scoff at royalty, imperialism, and the republic in turn, and to get rid of ideas, enthusiasms, and principles as readily as an actress gets rid of a worn dress.

It was done. Josephine had a new position. She was no more to be called Citizeness Bonaparte, but Madame, like the ladies of the old régime, until she should bear the title of Empress and Your Majesty. The Republic existed only in name; its institutions were gone. One man alone was left: Bonaparte as First Consul was more than a constitutional sovereign, and many queens possess less influence and prestige than

did his wife. Yet on the whole, the really republican
period of their lives was the happiest portion. Before
Brumaire Bonaparte counted for a soldier of liberty,
and his wife was deemed a truly patriotic woman.
All that time, she had served the interests of her ambitious husband with great intelligence. Without
her he would hardly have attained such wonderful
results. She it was who secured for him the support
of Barras, and had him made, when but twenty-six,
the commander-in-chief of the Army of Italy; at
Milan she was as useful to him as in Paris, by conciliating aristocratic society in both cities; during the
Directory, she allayed the jealousy of the Directory,
and made herself welcome to both Royalists and
Republicans; on the morning of the 18th Brumaire,
she covered his sword with flowers, and in her per-
fumed note laid a snare for Gohier. The movement
was irresistible; Madame Bonaparte's smiles completed her husband's work.

After the 18th Brumaire Lucien still nourished
liberal hopes, like Daunou, Cabanis, Grégoire, Carnot,
and Lafayette. He was sure that the Republic
would never turn into a monarchy, and sincerely
believed that he had saved liberty. Later, he said at
Saint Cyr to General Gouvion: "Will you not
acknowledge, dear General, that you knew this soldier, once your equal, now your Emperor, when he
was a sincere and ardent Republican? No, you will
say, he deceived us by false appearances. Well, for
my part, I will say that he deceived himself; for a

long time General Bonaparte was a Republican like
you or me. He served the Republic of the Convention with all the ardor which you saw, and as you
would not, perhaps, have dared to do yourself in such
a land, amid such a population. . . . The independent character of the sturdy mountaineers among
whom we were born taught him to respect human
dignity ; and it was only when the temporary consul-
ship was succeeded by the consulate for life, when a
sort of court grew up at the Tuileries, and Madame
Bonaparte was surrounded by prefects and ladies-in-
waiting, that any change could be detected in the
master's mind, and that he proceeded to treat everybody as everybody desired to be treated."

It was possibly in spite of himself that Napoleon
became a Cæsar. The evening of the 18th Brumaire
he still hoped to secure the consent of the two Councils and to avoid all illegality. Who knows ? If
the Directors had consented to lower the limit of age,
and to receive him as a colleague, although he was
not yet thirty, and the Constitution required that the
Directors should be forty years old, the *coup d'état*
might never have happened. On what things the
fate of republics and empires depends !

At first, Bonaparte was a Republican, and Josephine a Legitimist. As Emperor and Empress they
became Imperialists. But royal splendors cannot
make us forget the Republican period. The modest
uniform of the hero of Arcole was perhaps preferred
to the gorgeous coronation robes, and more than

once, beneath the golden hangings of the Imperial
palaces, Josephine regretted the modest house in the
rue de la Victoire, the sanctuary of her love. The
bright sun of the South could not make her forget the
first rays of dawn. Like France, she lost in liberty
what she gained in grandeur. A life of almost
absolute independence was followed by all the slavery
of the highest rank. She was already a queen except
in name. When she left her little house in the rue
de la Victoire a few days after the 18th Brumaire,
it was to take up her quarters in the Luxembourg.
But the residence of Maria de' Medici was not large
enough for the First Consul and Madame Bonaparte.
They went in a few days to take the place in the
Tuileries of the King and Queen of France, and
Lucien, the unwitting promoter of the Empire, was
to regret, as he put it, " that the Constitution of the
Consular Republic could have been so readily sacri-
ficed to what may be called the personification of the
monarchical power, which in the person of the unfor-
tunate Louis XVI., the best-meaning of sovereigns,
had been so barbarously destroyed." Madame Bonaparte was to be compelled to part company with Madame Tallien and several of her best friends of the society of the Directory. Even the name of Barras, once
so powerful, now obscure and forgotten in his estate of
Grosbois, was never to be uttered. Bonaparte could
not bear to be reminded that once he had been de-
pendent on that man. Already the herd of flatterers,
who were to form the consular court, had begun to

gather. The ideas and fashions of the past were about to reappear. Many Republican innovations did not outlaw the new almanac. A dead society came back to life. Madame Bonaparte appeared what she was in fact, though not to a careless observer, — a woman of the old régime. The Tuileries were not far from the Faubourg Saint Germain. But for all her success, her wealth, her greatness, Josephine could not recall the days of the Republic without emotion. Then she was young; and nothing can take the place of youth. Then she was powerful; and is not hope always sweeter than the reality? Then she was beautiful; and for a woman is not beauty the only true power? Then she was worshipped by her husband, and to appear charming in his eyes she did not need the splendor of the throne. In her plain dress of white muslin and a white flower in her hair, she seemed to him more beautiful than in her coronation robes of silver brocade covered with pink bees, and her crown sparkling with gems. She had no equerries, chamberlains, or maids of honor; but her youth adorned her more than a diadem. As Empress and Queen, Josephine was doubtless to regret the time when in a Republican society she bore no other title than that of Citizeness Bonaparte.

# INDEX.